RECRUITING: HOW TO DO IT

Other books by Iain Maitland:

How to Recruit
Managing Staff
The Barclays Guide to Managing Staff for the Small Business
Getting a Result: Managing People in the Small and Growing Business
Motivating People
How to Win at Job Hunting
How to Win at Interviews
Answer the Question: Get the Job!
Managing Your Time
Correct Letters
Tricky Business Forms
The Business Planner: A Complete Guide to Raising Finance
Budgeting for Non-financial Managers
How to Buy and Run a Shop
Franchising: a Practical Guide for Franchisers and Franchisees
Running a Successful Advertising Campaign
How to Plan Press Advertising
How to Plan Exhibitions
How to Plan Radio Advertising
How to Plan Direct Mail
The Perfect Conference
How to Organise a Conference
The Business Environment

Recruiting:
How to do it

Iain Maitland

CASSELL

Cassell
Wellington House, 125 Strand, London WC2R 0BB
http://www.cassell.co.uk

Distributed in USA by Cassell & Continuum
370 Lexington Avenue, New York, NY 10017-6550

First published 1997
Reprinted 1998

British Library Cataloguing-in-Publication Data
A catalogue record for this book is available from the British Library.

ISBN 0–304–33315–8 (paperback)

Designed and typeset by Kenneth Burnley at Irby, Wirral, Cheshire.
Printed and bound in Great Britain by Biddles Ltd, Guildford and King's Lynn

Contents

To Tracey, Michael and Sophie

List of figures

Preface

R*ECRUITING: HOW TO DO IT* is written for you – the personnel officer of a small, medium-sized or large business, who wants to approach recruitment in the correct professional manner. This book puts the whole process into its proper context – within the framework of a personnel plan, devised for up to a five-year period and amended on a regular, ongoing basis.

Chapter 1: 'Introducing a personnel plan' tells you how to create one for the first time – by understanding the role of personnel plans, assessing the current staff situation, identifying likely influences on staff requirements, recognizing probable changes to staffing levels and estimating the future staffing situation. Only then can a personnel plan be established.

Next, Chapter 2: 'Studying existing vacancies' looks at the initial stages of recruitment in relation to your plan – analyzing jobs that are vacant and composing job descriptions and person specifications, which are the two key documents used throughout recruitment and beyond, into employment. Discrimination, and how to avoid it, is examined too.

Chapter 3: 'Looking for applicants' considers the advantages and disadvantages of transferring and promoting from within the firm, and compares this with recruiting externally. It goes on to show you how to choose the most appropriate sources of recruitment in your circumstances, and how to advertise vacancies, both inside and outside the organization.

Then, Chapter 4: 'Shortlisting applicants' examines the various ways in which you can reduce a large pool of applicants to perhaps half a dozen candidates who can be interviewed – by distributing application forms, requesting letters with or without curricula vitae, and handling telephone calls. It proceeds to indicate how you should pick a screening method, and compose your shortlist.

Chapter 5: 'Interviewing candidates' details this key selection technique, explaining how to prepare for interviews, whatever their type, length, or location. It follows on by telling you how to begin, direct and end an interview, exchanging all of the information that you and the interviewee need.

Moving ahead, Chapter 6: 'Testing candidates' outlines the complex but increasingly important role of tests. It explains how to decide if you need to use tests, and whether or not to include individual and/or group tests within your selection procedures.

Chapter 7: 'Selecting employees' draws the recruitment and selection process to a close and shows you how to appraise the various candidates and come to a final decision before making a job offer to the most appropriate person. It also sets out how to induct the new employee into the organization, as quickly and efficiently as you can.

Probably most important of all, Chapter 8: 'Developing a personnel plan' tells you how to make the most of your plan throughout its term – by constantly evaluating staff needs and monitoring staffing levels at every opportunity. This will enable you to maintain the plan, and match needs and levels as closely as possible.

Of course, this is much more than a straightforward textbook. It is a workbook too, full of checklists, questionnaires and forms for completion. It is also a reference manual, containing examples of recruitment documents and letters, major codes of practice, useful contacts and recommended reading selections plus a glossary of key terms and phrases. It provides you with all you need to know about recruiting today – but for tomorrow's workforce.

Iain Maitland

Acknowledgements

I wish to thank the following organizations for giving me permission to reproduce their material in the book:

- Commission for Racial Equality
- Equal Opportunities Commission
- Department of Employment
- The Metropolitan Police

1 Introducing a personnel plan

Understanding personnel plans
Assessing the current situation
Identifying likely influences
Recognizing probable changes
Estimating the future position
Summary

I F YOU ARE TO INTRODUCE a personnel plan success-fully, you should begin by building up a fuller understanding of what it actually is *and* can do for you, before going on to compose one – by assessing the current situation, identifying influences, recognizing probable changes and estimating the future position.

Understanding personnel plans
Clearly, it is sensible to start by finding out as much as you can about personnel plans – most notably their role, benefits and drawbacks for your firm. Only then can you realistically expect to move ahead and be able to compile one which is absolutely relevant to your particular circumstances.

Their role
So, what exactly is a personnel – or 'manpower' – plan? It may be defined quite simply as 'a scheme whereby current and future staffing needs and levels are identified and worked towards with a view to ensuring they are matched as precisely as possible'. Typically, such a plan will be composed for up to a five-year period; any longer than that, and it is likely to become increasingly speculative, and therefore invalid.

Probably the main purpose of a personnel plan is to help a business to make the best use of its staff, by providing a framework against which it can recruit, train and develop, transfer and promote, dismiss and retire them, all at the most appropriate times. Hopefully, this will enable you to always have the right numbers and types of employees as and when required.

The benefits
If – and it is sometimes a big 'If' – a personnel plan is drawn up as carefully and as accurately as possible, then it can generate many advantages for your firm. It helps you to start recruiting effectively, as from *now*, selecting people not only for today's but for tomorrow's workforce too. Equally important, it enables you to compile a

long-term recruitment programme, as you will know which and how many employees are needed, where *and* when.

It allows you to prepare key staff in anticipation of transfers and promotions to other positions in due course. For example, training can be carried out as and when it is most appropriate, rather than at the last possible moment, or even after the new job has begun, which often happens. Also, it enables you to 'lose' unsuitable and/or excess staff via natural wastage such as moving away and retirement, rather than through dismissals or redundancies, which can be painful and costly procedures.

Furthermore, the existence of a personal plan may help you to avoid understaffing at any time which can leave staff overworked and feeling stressed and resentful, unable to cope with their demanding workload. Similarly, it can ensure that you eliminate overstaffing, whereby too many employees are chasing too little work, opportunities for career development are limited, and – of some significance – an excessive wage bill has to be met month in, month out.

It also enables you to keep abreast of ever-changing circumstances, and (hopefully) ahead of your competitors as well. An expanding or contracting industry, skills shortfalls in key areas, shortages and gluts of people of certain ages, new work patterns and so on will all affect the level and type of personnel required, and available. By planning ahead properly, you will know what the influences and changes are likely to be and can act accordingly *now,* leaving your rivals to react afterwards, when it may be too late to recruit the right numbers and types of people.

The drawbacks   Not surprisingly, a personnel plan does have some disadvantages. It is very hard to compile, with each of four, key stages having to be completed with considerable care and accuracy if the finalized plan is to be usable. You have to assess current staffing needs and levels, identify likely influences upon those needs, recognize probable changes in the levels and then analyze future staffing requirements and levels; and every stage is difficult to estimate and becomes harder to anticipate as you progress.

A careless and inaccurate plan – and the vast majority of personnel plans can be classified as such – is of little use. As an example, if you have not spotted and evaluated *all* of the possible influences on needs *and* changes of levels then it is impossible to appraise your future requirements with any degree of certainty. Indeed, an appropriate plan may be detrimental as it can mean the wrong numbers and types of employee are taken on. Typically, some will then have to be dismissed or made redundant at a later date because they are unsuitable or no longer needed, and this is an unpleasant and expensive matter.

It is more important to bear in mind that a carefully composed personnel plan will need to be monitored and evaluated, amended and even wholly revised on an ongoing basis – again, no easy task, and with plenty of opportunities for errors to be made. External influences upon staffing needs – most notably technological change and its rate of development – cannot be estimated accurately. People are notoriously unpredictable: they resign because of a better job offer or to move away if their partner is transferred elsewhere. Some will become sick and have to take early retirement. Sadly, others will die unexpectedly.

Evidently, you need to adopt a relatively flexible approach to your plan. It provides you with a framework to work within and towards but it should be loose and fluid, changing regularly according to circumstances. Too rigid, inflexible and followed too closely, and you will inevitably find that as time progresses, the wrong types and numbers of people will be employed by your firm, with all of the problems which that entails: poor workrate and performance, low productivity, ill feeling and tension amongst them. Look on your plan as a set of guidelines rather than rules.

Assessing the current situation
The first stage of compiling a first-class personnel plan consists of three separate but inter-related activities – calculating your present staff needs, comparing these with existing staffing levels and making adjustments to ensure that they become as similar as possible.

Present staff needs
To begin with, you should consider the quantity and quality of staff needed by your firm – typically in terms of the total number required, the numbers for each department, the roles of those people within the departments, and the skills, knowledge and experience to do the jobs properly. To calculate requirements, you really need to have access to the organization's trading figures, most specifically in terms of both production and sales. Also, you must be able to work closely with heads of department who are conscious of the overall workload they are responsible for, how it should be divided up and allocated, and the number and types of people required to do it.

Existing staffing levels
It is then sensible to look at your existing workforce – the total numbers in the business and different departments, their grades and functions, age, sex, skills, knowledge, experience, qualifications and length of service, in particular. This information should be readily available to you, predominantly from recruitment and selection documents such as completed application forms and curricula vitae, employment documents like personnel records and performance appraisal forms, and from departmental and company literature such as organization charts. Whatever you use, do make sure it is up to date. Many documents – especially organization charts – do age very quickly indeed.

Making adjustments Similarly, you need to start making some adjustments to your workforce as and where necessary to try to match it up as closely as you can to your current requirements. Perhaps there are too few employees in one department and you have to recruit – either externally or internally, by transferring or promoting from within other, potentially overstaffed departments. Alternatively, some members of staff may be the wrong types, short of specific skills and expertise and in need of training and development. Possibly, there are too many employees in a certain department, who can either be moved elsewhere if they have the necessary abilities or, as a last resort, manoeuvred out of the firm, preferably on a voluntary basis.

Identifying likely influences Aware of your current staff needs, you then have to press on to look at the likely influences upon them over a forthcoming period of time, most probably three to five years. The identification and understanding of these influences will consequently help you to work out your future staff requirements during the coming months and years. Influences may be divided into two categories: internal and external ones.

Internal influences Inevitably, the firm's overall objectives will have a huge impact on the numbers and types of staff needed. The business may intend to expand, increasing production or boosting sales by opening other outlets so that more employees are needed, perhaps with similar skills to the existing ones. It could be planning to diversify into other product or geographical markets. Thus, more workers will again be required, but more likely with a different mix of skills and expertise. Alternatively, the business might be expecting to have to fight to retain its present market share against rising competition, or even to contract in the foreseeable future, with the loss of jobs becoming a strong possibility.

Perhaps the business may have plans to restructure its organization in some way – to merge its finance and administration departments into one, to separate the marketing department into two, with an advertising and promotions section, or to change from a functional to a divisional structure. All of these plans will affect the numbers and types of personnel needed. Clearly, you have to be conscious of what is happening (and going to happen) internally, by checking memos, attending meetings and studying departmental and corporate plans, if available. Figure 1.1 is a checklist of some of the other, internal influences which need to be considered.

External influences Similarly, it is wise to be aware of current and developing external influences upon your concern, and the size and make-up of its workforce. Typically, your trade or industry may be shrinking, remaining static or expanding, which could have

There are many internal influences upon staff needs, including the following. As with all subsequent checklists, you may find it helpful to think about each topic and its effects before ticking the appropriate box as a reminder, and moving on to the next one. See this as a provisional list. Add to it if you can.

Organizational policies	
Organizational strategies	
Organizational objectives	
Purchasing plans	
Production plans	
Research and development plans	
Marketing plans	
Market research plans	
Sales plans	
Financial plans	
Administration plans	
Personnel plans	
Organizational structure	
Management practices	
Work organization methods	
Staff flexibility	
Productivity	
Equipment and machinery	
Computerization	
Technology	
Others?	

Figure 1.1: A checklist of internal influences on staff needs

knock-on effects on your firm and its employees. The economic environment may be changing for better or worse. Perhaps interest rates are rising rapidly which might make your business reluctant to borrow money in order to finance an expansion programme. Possibly, inflation is increasing too, which could mean that your goods are becoming less competitive in the international marketplace, and output (and therefore manpower) needs to be reduced for the foreseeable future.

The political situation may alter in the forthcoming months and years, with new policies encouraging or discouraging expansion. Technology – almost inevitably – will improve substantially during the term of the personnel plan, often resulting in fewer but more specialized employees being required to operate updated equipment and machinery. You must remain aware of these developments, studying trade magazines and reports, attending seminars and conferences, reading widely, and generally keeping on top of wider, ever-changing business issues. Some of the other, external influences which need to be taken into account are shown in the checklist reproduced as Figure 1.2 (pages 8 to 9).

Recognizing probable changes   Whilst identifying likely influences upon your staff needs, it is sensible to try to recognize the probable changes in your staffing levels over the same period of time, three to five years. Like the influences, changes can be classified in two ways: internal and (perhaps less obviously) external ones.

Internal changes   Studying your present workforce, calculate who is going to go where, and when. Paying particular attention to such matters as age, sex, position in the firm and length of service, contemplate who is most likely to retire, leave perhaps to raise a family or move elsewhere because of a partner's promotion and resign, possibly because they have advanced as far as they can in the organization. Think about who can be trained and developed, transferred or promoted into different posts to cover these departures. You should be able to draw conclusions by looking at labour turnover figures to date, as well as through talking to employees, colleagues and heads of department, as relevant.

External changes   Often overlooked when piecing together a personnel plan, it is worthwhile looking outside the firm at the labour market from which you will (hopefully) draw the right numbers and types of employee. Consider its size and composition. Perhaps some parts of it are dwindling – school leavers, for example – which suggests your firm may have to work extra hard and offer more to attract the right people. Possibly, other parts of the market do not possess the skills that you need in your concern. As an example, science graduates may not only be in short supply, but could lack the necessary, practical know-how required to do what you want. It may be more sensible to train internally, rather than recruit externally.

Just as important, you should be familiar with the trends that are developing within the labour market – most notably, school leavers staying on longer in further education, an increased number of (part-time) working mothers, the growing demand for job sharing, flexi-time, working from home, early retirement, and so on. Not surprisingly, these will all affect your firm – it will need to offer a revised employment package to people, if it wants to recruit them. Whether recruiting locally, nationally or internationally, job centres, local authorities and the Department of Employment will be able to supply data on such external developments. Figure 1.3 (page 10) is a checklist highlighting other common employment trends of the 1990s.

Estimating the future position   Conscious of your current situation, likely influences upon needs and probable changes in levels, you can set about analyzing the future position in three to five years. You must estimate future staff needs and levels, and then create an ongoing plan so that these are matched as closely as possible at all times throughout that period.

Future staffing needs   Having considered internal influences such as corporate objectives, and external ones like the economic environment (as well as any other influences that are relevant to your firm), you should be able to assess the numbers and types of employees required over the forthcoming period of time. Attempt to classify your estimated requirements in terms of the total number, the numbers per department, the roles of each employee, and the skills, knowledge and experience needed to carry out all of these jobs. Double-check your assessment against the firm's anticipated trading figures, and with the heads of department whom you have been liaising with.

Forthcoming staffing levels   Likewise, having studied all of the probable internal changes involving retirements and resignations and the external ones including skills shortages and developing employment trends (plus any other changes that are of significance to your concern), you ought to be in a position to appreciate the size and make-up of your future workforce. Try to categorize employees with regard to the total numbers in the business and different departments, grades and functions, age and sex, skills, knowledge, experience, qualifications and length of employment. You may find it helpful to sketch out a revised organization chart, and to talk again to department heads, as and when appropriate.

Staff needs can be affected by innumerable external factors, such as these. There may be others you can incorporate into the list, some of which may be specific to your particular situation. View this as an initial list, to be built upon.

Your trade or industry	– growth?	
	– decline?	
Suppliers	– availability?	
	– supplies?	
	– cost of materials?	
Customers	– growth?	
	– decline?	
	– demand for goods?	
Competitors	– growth?	
	– decline?	
	– expansion?	
	– mergers?	
	– acquisitions?	
	– strategies?	
The economy	– interest rates?	
	– inflation?	
	– employment levels?	
	– unemployment levels?	
The state	– local government?	
	– national government?	
	– international government?	
The law	– trade bodies' codes?	
	– local government?	
	– national government?	
	– international government?	

The population	– age?	
	– structure?	
	– skills?	
	– attitudes?	
Society	– culture?	
	– customs?	
	– fashions?	
The environment	– concerns?	
	– pressures?	
The international marketplace	– exchange rates?	
	– import rates?	
	– export regulations?	
	– tariffs?	
	– embargoes?	
	– blockades?	
	– treaties?	
	– wars?	
Other		

Figure 1.2: *A checklist of external influences on staff needs*

Many different employment trends have become apparent in the 1990s and it is sensible to be aware of the main ones, especially these. Consider how they affect you, and your plan.

The labour force is expanding in age, but changing in structure	
A smaller number of young people now exist	
Youngsters remain in further education for much longer	
An increased number of women are available for work	
More women return to work after having children	
A larger number of people from ethnic groups are seeking employment	
More self-employed people exist	
An increased number of older people are active in the jobs market	
The labour force is also changing in terms of the skills on offer	
Skills shortfalls exist in (a) certain occupations	
(b) some trades and industries	
(c) various regions	
Skills gluts occur in (a) some occupations	
(b) various trades and industries	
(c) certain regions	
The labour force is changing its attitudes to work arrangements	
Part-time work is more popular than ever before	
Temporary and freelance work is in demand	
Job sharing satisfies two or more people	
Flexi-time is fashionable nowadays	
Term-time working often suits working mothers	
Working from home is increasingly popular	
Career breaks are demanded by many working mothers	
Early retirement is becoming the norm: at 50 or 55	

Figure 1.3: *A checklist of employment trends in the 1990s*

Creating a plan   Knowing what you are likely to require in terms of the quantity and quality of employees, *and* what you will probably have, you can put together a plan to make sure they are as similar as possible. Evidently, recruitment – both externally and internally through transfers and promotion – is the driving force behind such a plan as it should ensure that you take on and employ the right numbers and types of people in the right places, *and* at the right times. Hopefully, your successful recruitment processes will be supported by ongoing training and development as and where appropriate, and voluntary resignations and retirements, wherever necessary. A personnel plan is reproduced in Figure 1.4 (page 12); you should be able to use this for the firm, each department and different types of employee.

SUMMARY   **1.** A personnel plan is a scheme whereby current and future staffing needs and levels are identified and worked towards with a view to ensuring they are matched as precisely as possible. It may be composed for up to a five-year period.

2. To compile an effective plan, it is sensible to begin by assessing the current situation: in particular, present staff needs and existing staffing levels. Adjustments can then be made to bring these into line with each other.

3. Next, likely influences upon staff needs have to be identified. These influences can be categorized in two ways – internal and external ones. All influences must be considered fully and carefully.

4. Then, probable changes to staff levels need to be recognized. These can be classified as internal changes within the workforce and external ones to the labour market. Again, these must be studied, comprehensively and in a conscientious manner.

5. Finally, the future position can be analyzed in terms of both future staff needs and forthcoming staffing levels. Consequently, a personnel plan can be created and adhered to – albeit on a loose and flexible basis.

	Year to	Year to	Year to	Year to
Opening staff needs				
Changes during year				
Total staff needs				
Opening staff levels				
Additions from transfers and promotions				
Losses from transfers and promotion				
Losses from natural wastage				
Losses from retirement				
Total staff levels				
Balance (staff needs/staff levels)				
Additions required				
Losses required				

Figure 1.4: *A personnel plan form*

2 Studying existing vacancies

Analyzing jobs
Composing job descriptions
Compiling person specifications
Avoiding discrimination
Summary

INEVITABLY, YOUR PERSONNEL PLAN will have revealed – if you did not already know about – a number of existing or imminent vacancies, perhaps resulting from understaffing, or because someone is due to leave, to be transferred or promoted, or to retire. Accordingly, these vacancies may have to be filled in accordance with the plan, whether from outside or inside the organization. The preliminary stages of recruiting the right people consist of analyzing jobs, composing job descriptions, compiling person specifications and – of some significance – making sure that you avoid discriminating during these *and* all subsequent procedures.

Analyzing jobs Job analysis might be described as 'the systematic process of accumulating information about and appraising all aspects of a given job'. Whether you are seeking to fill an existing job which is vacant or about to become vacant, or a soon-to-be-created one, you need to consider job analysis in terms of its purpose, the information required and how to gather and then assess that information properly.

Its purpose Job analysis, when carried out in such a way that you know the particular job as if it were your own, is absolutely vital because successful recruitment develops directly from it. If you know that job inside out you can go on to amend it and/or those around it, so that they all fit together in line with your personnel plan. It also provides you with the detailed information needed to write job descriptions and person specifications which can then be used as guidelines when advertising, drafting application forms, screening applicants, interviewing candidates *and* beyond, into employment. Quite simply, if you do not know that job extremely well, you cannot possibly expect to be able to fill it with the most suitable person.

The information You need to find out anything and everything you can
required about each job – in particular, its overall purpose and
objectives, type (whether temporary, part-time or full-
time), position and the superiors, colleagues, subordinates and other
departments which the holder comes into contact with on an occasional, semi-
occasional or regular basis. As significant, you should be aware of its transfer
and promotion prospects and the likely length of its existence. Check on its
physical location within the organization and its work environment as this
affects the quantity and the quality of the work completed.

Furthermore, do be conscious of the authority
involved with the job, its main tasks and responsibilities (and whether these
are pleasant or unpleasant, easy or difficult), the work systems to be followed,
and the monitoring, measuring and assessment procedures which exist. Equally relevant, contemplate the skills, knowledge and experience needed by the
job holder to perform each task and duty and the job itself well. Figure 2.1
(pages 16 and 17) is a questionnaire which you may wish to complete during
the job analysis process.

Gathering It should be relatively easy to gather together all of the
information key information required, especially if the job has
existed for some time. You may have done it personal-
ly in the past or are presently watching it being carried out by the current job
holder, on a day-to-day basis. Thus, you may be able to answer many of the
questions about the job yourself, from your hands-on knowledge. Company
documents such as organization charts, staff appraisal forms and the personnel plan itself can be referred to as well – although it is important to check that
these are up-to-date and relevant.

If the present job holder is about to be moved or is to
leave – and is happy about this and therefore receptive to an approach – you
can interview him or her about different aspects of the work. Just as beneficial
– if not more so if the job is about to be created – employees in the same or similar employment may be spoken to. They could also keep work diaries, setting
down exactly what they do each day, when, how and why. Superiors, colleagues
and subordinates can be drawn into conversation too, perhaps being asked
comparable questions to those listed in the questionnaire shown as Figure 2.1.

Assessing Once you have accumulated all of your notes, and per-
information haps transferred them onto an easy-to-read form such
as the one given in Figure 2.2 (pages 18 and 19), then
you can assess each job more carefully; this time in relation to your personnel
plan. Always remember that this is the framework against which you are
recruiting (and subsequently training, developing and so forth). Make sure you
are convinced it should continue – perhaps it duplicates other jobs, overlaps
with their tasks and responsibilities or is going to cease to exist shortly, possibly after reorganization. Decide whether or not it still has a place in the firm.

If it does, contemplate whether it should carry on in its present form; possibly, a full-time job could be streamlined onto a compact and cost-conscious part-time basis, with some activities being reallocated, and an employee being used to cover only the busiest working periods. Perhaps certain parts of the job-holder's authority, tasks and responsibilities would be better placed elsewhere, to enable this and other jobs to fit in well, and blend together better than before. Addressing this issue will help you to reach decisions about each particular job, to make certain that it continues (if appropriate) in keeping with the overall personnel plan.

Composing job descriptions Following on from your job analysis, you can compose job descriptions for each of the remaining jobs to be filled. A job description is a document which outlines the main purpose, tasks and responsibilities of a job and is based upon all or some of the information gathered together during the job analysis process. You should be aware of the uses of such a document, and know something of its contents and style, so that you can compose them successfully.

Its uses A job description has many uses, especially during recruitment procedures. It will help you to focus on the precise skills, knowledge and expertise needed to perform the various tasks and responsibilities (and therefore the job itself) well. You can also use it as a source of reference when drafting advertisements and application forms, as it will indicate the points that should be stated and the questions which need to be asked, as appropriate. It can be handed over or sent out with application forms so that prospective applicants can decide if this is the job for them. If it is not, they will not apply, saving you the time and money which would have been spent on reading their applications and perhaps even interviewing them.

When studying application forms, letters, curricula vitae and/or talking on the telephone, you can compare and contrast previous work experience with the tasks and responsibilities involved with this job which may enable you to reject or select people for an interview. During interviews, it can be used for reference purposes, perhaps when you want to describe what the job entails, or ask candidates what they would do in a typical work situation. Should you wish to assess candidates further, work-related tests can be devised which are linked as closely as possible to the activities set out in the job description.

Once a person has been recruited externally or transferred or promoted from within, a job description continues to have several other, equally important uses. In particular, you can refer to it when a recruit is settling in, to show him or her exactly what is involved, Similarly, it (or the job description for the next job up the line) can be implemented into training and development programmes, acting as a checklist to work against and towards. Again, you can refer to it during the appraisal, grievance, disciplinary

*Answering all of the following questions should give you a full and complete under-
standing of the job being analyzed.*

What is the job title?   _____

What is its main purpose?   _____

What are its objectives?   _____

                                               _____

                                               _____

Is it a temporary, part- or

full-time job?   _____

Referring to an organization chart,

where does it fit in?   _____

Who does the job holder answer to? _____

Who is the job holder in charge of? _____

Who does he or she deal with

regularly, semi-regularly and

occasionally?   _____

                                               _____

                                               _____

What are the job holder's transfer

prospects?   _____

What are his or her promotion

prospects?   _____

                                               _____

How long is the job expected to

last for?   _____

Where exactly is the job located? _____

What is the work environment like? _____

What authority does the job holder

have?   _____

What are the tasks and

responsibilities of the job?   _____

(a) How are these carried out? _____

_____

(b) Which are easy (e)? _____

(c) Which are difficult (d)? _____

(d) Which are physically

demanding (pd)? _____

(e) Which are mentally

demanding (md)? _____

(f) Which are emotionally

demanding (ed)? _____

What work standards are expected?_____

_____

_____

How is the work monitored,

measured and assessed? _____

_____

_____

What skills are needed to

do the job? _____

_____

_____

What knowledge is required to

do the job? _____

_____

_____

What experience is needed to

do the job? _____

_____

_____

Figure 2.1: A job analysis questionnaire

JOB ANALYSIS FORM

Job title:	Responsible to:
Department:	Responsible for:

Purpose and objectives:

Position and contacts:

Work environment:

Authority, tasks and responsibilities:

Work standards and checking procedures:

Skills, knowledge and experience:

Job prospects::

Name:	Job title:
Signature:	Date:

Figure 2.2: A job analysis form

and even dismissal interviews, to highlight shortcomings and, if necessary , the reasons for dismissal.

Its contents   The information included in a job description will vary enormously from one document to another – not just because each job is unique but also as a result of the different approaches and attitudes which prevail in organizations. Some descriptions will be no more than a skeleton framework of points, whilst others are enormously complex and detailed. Whatever your preference, you should at least set down the appropriate job titles of the holder and his or her superiors and subordinates as well as the main purpose, tasks and responsibilities of the job, plus its future prospects. As the composer of the job description, your job title, name, signature and the date should conclude the document. An example of a job description is shown as Figure 2.3. Yours may be more detailed.

Taking each heading in turn, the 'Job title' must be clear and straightforward – as an example 'Shelf stacker' rather than 'Supermarket assistant'. A vague in-house job title used in advertisements can confuse and mislead readers, and as a consequence, suitable ones may decide not to apply whilst unsuitable ones do. The job titles of superiors and subordinates (if appropriate) should be stated under 'Responsible to' and 'Responsible for'. These must be self-explanatory. Avoid using real names – Mike James, Sophie Lewis, or whatever – as these people may change jobs shortly, thus outdating the document straight away.

The 'Purpose', 'Tasks' and 'Responsibilities' of the job must focus on the key ones – a lengthy list can bewilder your colleagues who might be responsible for drafting job advertisements or application forms, or conducting interviews. They may not know which are most and least significant, and could focus on the wrong ones. An endless list is off-putting for would-be applicants too, who may feel overwhelmed by everything that appears to need to be done. Use simple and precise language when describing tasks and responsibilities – not everyone understands jargon and slang expressions and may feel intimidated and put off by them.

Worth mentioning as a separate point as it is vitally important but often overlooked: do add a 'catch-all' phrase after the purpose, tasks and responsibilities have been stated. A sentence such as 'To carry out any other work as and when directed' or 'To complete other activities as instructed by the immediate superior' effectively incorporates all of those minor tasks and responsibilities which may have to be attended to from time to time. Adding such a phrase, referring to and explaining it at some stage – typically during a selection interview – will help to avoid disagreements later on about what is and what is not involved in the job.

'Future prospects' are rarely incorporated into a job description but should be because they need to work their way through into advertisements to attract applicants, and to be talked about during interviews. When in employment, the employee also has something tangible to target and

JOB DESCRIPTION

Job title: *Office assistant*

Responsible to: *Office manager*

Responsible for: *Not appropriate*

Purpose: *To assist the office manager as required*

Tasks and responsibilities:
To distribute incoming correspondence to the appropriate person or department

To photocopy and file copies of incoming correspondence

To type correspondence as instructed

To despatch outgoing correspondence

To photocopy and file copies of outgoing correspondence

To maintain office stationery supplies

To keep the office tidy

To run errands as directed

To carry out any other duties as instructed by the office manager

Future prospects:
Possible promotion to bought ledger or purchase ledger sections in 18-24 months, subject to satisfactory progress and work opportunities

Name: *Nicola Platek*		**Job title:** *Personnel Officer*	
Signature: *J. Smith*		**Date:** *2nd December 1996*	

Figure 2.3: *A job description*

work towards. Evidently, these prospects should be realistic, to avoid discouragement, ill feeling and even resignations at a later stage. Do round off the document with your job title, name and signature so that other people know who compiled it and who to refer to in case of queries. Put the date as well so they can see how relevant and up-to-date it is when they come to read it.

Its style   Of course, the individual style of a job description will differ quite considerably from others. Nonetheless, some guidelines do exist, and all documents should be compiled with these in mind. Your description must contain a broad range and number of relevant facts – enough to give everyone who looks at it a fairly full and complete impression of what is involved, including its attractive *and* less attractive features. It is imperative that all of the information stated is scrupulously accurate otherwise disputes and disagreements may develop between you and the relevant employee as and when he or she starts work.

Equally significant, all of the details given must be easy to understand – clear and self-explanatory job titles, simply and precisely explained tasks and responsibilities, and the like. Otherwise, colleagues who do not know the job as well as you may become confused, and prospective applicants could be misled. As a general rule – and rules are always there to be broken – a job description should ideally be about two, A4 pages long; much more than that and it is less likely to be read and absorbed, used as a checklist, a quick source of reference, or whatever.

Compiling person specifications   A 'person', 'employee', 'job' or 'personnel' specification' – to use a variety of common names – is inevitably compiled and used alongside the job description from which it is derived. Quite simply, this is a 'document which sets out the skills, knowledge and experience needed to do a particular job properly'. Again, you should be conscious of its possible uses as well as its contents and style, so that you can piece them together, as and when required.

Its uses   A person specification is perhaps most useful during recruitment processes. If you know who you want, it will help you to decide where to look for the 'ideal employee', either internally or externally, possibly head-hunting someone from another firm, or recruiting from the ranks of the unemployed. You can refer to it when drawing up job advertisements and application forms, to make certain that the correct points are made and questions asked. Never supply a copy of the specification to prospective applicants though – as some naïve recruiters have been known to do – because this will obviously enable them to pretend to be the type of person you are seeking.

Keeping the document to yourself and looking at it alongside the completed application forms, letters and curricula vitae or when talking to someone on the telephone, you can contrast applicants' skills, knowledge and experience with those of the 'perfect employee', thus rejecting or selecting them for the interview, as relevant. At an interview, it may be used as a checklist of points to be covered and discussed or questions to be raised, or even as an assessment form to be ticked, crossed or graded, as appropriate. If you intend to use tests, suitable ones can be selected by studying the specification and deciding which attributes can best be measured by testing, rather than interviewing; typically their specific aptitudes, such as manual dexterity.

The person specification still has a role to play *after* someone has been recruited, transferred or promoted into position. Predominantly, it acts as a yardstick during training and development programmes to see how well the employee is progressing towards the ideal. Similarly, it is used in this way during staff appraisal interviews, where performance is monitored and assessed, usually on an annual or bi-annual basis. As with the job description, it can also be incorporated into grievance, disciplinary and dismissal interviews to show weaknesses and reasons for the termination of employment.

Its contents   The contents of a person specification will vary considerably according to the job, and the individual approach of the organization. Nevertheless, all specifications should be compiled in exactly the same way: by looking at the purpose, tasks, responsibilities and future prospects listed in the job description and then calculating which qualities are needed to complete each of these properly. From this, an identikit picture of the perfect employee can be built up, typically under such headings as physical characteristics, achievements, personality, abilities, interests and general circumstances. Figure 2.4 (page 24) is an example of a person specification, which has been developed from the preceding job description shown as Figure 2.3 (pages 20–21). Yours may be more detailed.

Looking at these headings in sequence, 'Physical characteristics' would cover such areas as appearance, speech, health, eyesight, hearing, age, sex, race and disability. Appearance and speech may be significant if the person has to work with customers, but could be less relevant (or arguably irrelevant) if they do not. Good health – subject to the demands of the job – is always important, as you do not want your employees to be off sick regularly. Eyesight and hearing may be an issue, especially if the work is intricate or potentially hazardous. Age can be relevant if the job involves selling alcohol or adult videos for example, but perhaps should not otherwise act as a barrier. Sex, race and disability are inevitably contentious matters – you must not discriminate on these grounds.

'Achievements' will encompass topics such as education, qualifications, training and work experience. You may feel it is essential that the ideal employee has been educated to a certain standard, perhaps A-level, degree level or beyond. Be careful here though: employing an under-qualified person may mean he or she is incapable of doing the job, but an

PERSON SPECIFICATION

Job title: *Office assistant*

Physical characteristics: *Clean and tidy appearance (essential)*

Achievements: *4 GCSEs, 'C' grades or above (essential)*
English Language and Mathematics (desirable)
(Equivalent qualifications are acceptable)

Personality: *Friendly and outgoing nature (essential)*

Abilities: *Able to type at 50 words per minute (essential)*

Interests: *None of note*

General circumstances: *Able to work occasionally in the evenings and on*
Saturday mornings (essential)

Name: *Nicola Platek*	Job title: *Personnel Officer*
Signature: *J. Smith.*	Date: *2nd December 1996*

Figure 2.4: A person specification

overqualified one could become bored easily, and resign! It is wise to be flexible about the precise qualifications gained or training undertaken. For example, an applicant who has studied abroad may have different but equally valid certificates. Similarly, try not to be too rigid about previous work experience – key skills and expertise could have been acquired in other ways. As an example, applicants may have learned much from belonging to clubs and societies, organizing charity events, or whatever.

Difficult though it is to measure the traditional application form–interview–reference sequence, the 'Personality' of the perfect employee should be set out in the specification. The exact type of personality you are seeking will naturally vary although most employers probably look for fairly similar features: maturity, a calm and methodical manner, common sense, tact, a sense of humour and a team spirit. As these are relatively hard to assess accurately, tests are now being used more regularly as part of the selection process, particularly in larger organizations.

'Abilities' are equally tricky to appraise given the rather artificial nature of the recruitment sequence. Nevertheless, you may believe that the 'right' person should have certain abilities if they are to do the job competently. Typically, these might include a retentive memory, a broad and diverse general knowledge, verbal, numerical or literary talents and/or manual or mechanical aptitudes. Again, tests are being used more often during selection procedures in order to assess these aspects with greater accuracy and reliability.

Often overlooked when piecing together a person specification, 'Interests' can have an impact on someone's ability to do the work successfully. For example, running a club or society or arranging its activities might suggest a person has organizational skills which may be relevant to the job. Likewise, if he or she plays football or hockey then this would probably be an advantage if the job involves selling sports goods and equipment. Social, literary, artistic, sporting and other interests taking place out of working hours in a person's own time can be identified fairly easily by reading about them in application forms and talking to people in interviews.

The final, all-purpose heading should be called 'General circumstances' (or something similar), and acts as a catch-all for any other criteria you can think of that are relevant to this specific job. Perhaps the ideal person must have his or her own transport, a clean driving licence or should live in or close to a particular area. You may be able to think of other points which are especially appropriate to the job you are planning to fill. These may occur to you as you check each statement on the job description, in turn.

Its style Inevitably, there are some do's and don'ts to take account of when compiling a person specification: it is not enough to simply think of a lengthy list of key attributes needed and put them down on paper! Don't be too idealistic, setting so many requirements that you are unable to find such a perfect person – obviously, the more you set, the harder it will be to recruit someone. Do separate out the chosen attributes into 'essentials' and 'desirables' – those that the person must have and should have, if possible. 'Contra-indicators', such as a driving ban or a criminal record, can be included too, whereby applicants will automatically be rejected if these exist.

Do make certain that essential and desirable requirements (and any contra-indicators) can be measured and assessed easily, typically by studying application forms, letters and curricula vitae, interviewing candidates and taking up references perhaps from former employers. Requirements relating to outside interests, appearance and speech and previous work experience would fall into this category. Some are harder to assess, most notably a person's health and specific aptitudes. These will have to be evaluated by medical examination or various tests which may not be readily available, and are time-consuming and costly to arrange.

Don't be vague when listing your various requirements in your specification. Words like 'average', 'good', 'nice' and 'acceptable' are largely meaningless, because everyone defines them differently – a 'good' education means five GCSEs to some people; a 2:1 degree to others. If these words find their way into a job advertisement, an increased number of unsuitable people are likely to apply, wasting everyone's time and money. Likewise, if your colleagues help out with reading application forms and interviewing candidates – as often happens – you may find yourself with an employee who they consider 'good' but you think is 'absolutely awful'!

Don't discriminate when drawing up a person specification, or indeed at any other time in the recruitment process, or thereafter during employment. In particular, it is illegal to discriminate on the grounds of sex, marital status and race: to do so could lead to a complaint to an industrial tribunal. If upheld, your firm might have to pay financial compensation and could also receive unwelcome media attention, potentially unsettling your present workforce, dissuading prospective applicants from applying for future vacancies, and offending your customers too. Try to avoid discriminating unfairly in any way – physical disability, age, and sexual preference rarely (if ever) affect a person's ability to do a job, and everyone deserves to be judged by this rather than another person's prejudices.

Avoiding discrimination

Various Acts have been passed which attempt to eliminate or at least much reduce unlawful discrimination, and these include the Sex Discrimination Act 1975, the Race Relations Act 1976 and the Disabled Persons (Employment) Act 1958. Specific legislation has not yet been passed to minimize discrimination on the basis of age and/or sexual preferences, although the points made in relation to the existing Acts should enable you to monitor yourself in these respects as well.

The Sex Discrimination Act 1975 It is illegal to discriminate against people on the grounds of their sex or marital status with regard to the arrangements for filling a vacancy, deciding who should be offered the post and the conditions of employment given. Once employed, staff are entitled to equal access and on the same terms to any facilities, services and benefits, training and development and transfers and promotions. They must not be sexually harassed, receive any unfavourable treatment, be selected for redundancy nor be dismissed for discriminatory reasons. The Act applies to women *and* men, full-, part-time and temporary employees and self-employed people contracted to do work, all regardless of their length of employment.

Unlawful discrimination can be either 'direct' or 'indirect'. 'Direct discrimination' takes place when one person is treated less favourably than another of the opposite sex or marital status would be in the same or similar circumstances. As an example, only male applicants are recruited for what the firm considers to be 'a man's job', such as a car mechanic or labourer. 'Indirect discrimination' exists when requirements or conditions are established which tend to favour people of a particular sex or marital status more than another. For example, a minimum height and/or weight requirement is set for a labouring job. On reflection, this can be seen to favour men, as they tend to be taller and heavier than women.

There are various exceptions to the Act. Sex discrimination is lawful in recruitment, training and development and access to transfers and promotions if sex is a 'genuine occupational qualification'. A person of a particular sex may be required for authenticity, to preserve privacy or dignity when the organization provides care and attention for people of only one sex or when the job involves providing personal services regarding education or welfare and which are best supplied by one sex. Other exceptions relate to certain jobs in private households, the prison service, the police and armed forces. See Appendix A (page 121) for more information about sex discrimination, and how to avoid it.

The Race Relations Act 1976 In many respects, the essence of this is the same as the Sex Discrimination Act: it is unlawful to discriminate against people because of their colour, race, nationality or ethnic origin. This applies from recruitment through training, development, transfers and promotions and on to dismissals and redundancy situations. All racial groups have a right to equal access, opportunity, and terms and conditions at all times, regardless of their type of work, the number of hours worked or the length of their employment.

Again, illegal discrimination can be categorized in two ways: 'direct' and 'indirect'. Only ever promoting white employees into managerial positions may indicate that direct discrimination is occurring. Demanding a high standard of spoken English in order to do a job might be viewed as indirect discrimination because a smaller number of people from certain racial groups will be able to meet the requirement.

There are some exceptions to this Act. Selection on racial grounds is permitted for jobs where it is a 'genuine occupational qualification', most notably for reasons of authenticity. For example, a model or an actor may need to be of a particular racial group. Also, the Act does not cover employment in private households or in the Civil Service. Appendix B (page 125) details racial discrimination more fully, and tells you how to avoid it.

The Disabled Persons (Employment) Act 1958 Under this Act, a voluntary register of disabled people was set up. If you have a workforce of twenty or more people, you have a duty to employ a quota of these registered, disabled people. The quota is currently set at three per cent of your total workforce. Although it is not a legal offence to be below quota, you should try to recruit suitable registered disabled people if they are available as and when vacancies arise. If you wish to employ an able-bodied person, then you should obtain a permit to do so from the local job centre.

The Act also has the power to designate certain jobs – such as lift and car park attendants – for registered disabled people, if they are available. Employers with over twenty employees and/or designated jobs are obliged to keep records showing the number and names of people employed along with their starting and finishing dates of employment. These records should also identify registered disabled employees, those employed by permit and/or in designated employment. Refer to Appendix C (page 128) for further information on this topic, to ensure that you act in a fair and proper manner.

Clearly, avoiding discrimination is an important issue which should be considered throughout the introduction *and* development of your personnel plan. There are three organizations which are especially active in this field: the Equal Opportunities Commission, the Commission for Racial Equality and the Department of Employment are all committed to working towards the elimination of discrimination and the promotion of equality of opportunity. Their respective Codes of Practice effectively act as checklists for avoiding discrimination at all times and are thus reproduced by kind permission as Appendices A, B and C at the end of the text.

SUMMARY 1. Job analysis is the systematic process of accumulating information about and appraising all aspects of a given job. It is important to gather up as much data from as many sources, and to assess it as fully as possible, as successful recruitment develops from this initial analysis.

2. A job description is a document outlining the main purpose, tasks and responsibilities of a job, and can be used throughout recruitment and employment –

assuming that it contains sufficient detailed and accurate facts, laid out in an easy to understand style.

3. A person specification is a document which sets out the skills, knowledge and experience needed to do a particular job properly. Like the job description, it can be referred to during recruitment and employment, if it includes relevant contents, all stated in a clear and accessible style.

4. Various Acts have been passed which prohibit unlawful discrimination with regard to sex, race or disability. These must be understood and adhered to. Discrimination on the grounds of age or sexual preferences should ideally be avoided too. A person's ability to do the job is – or certainly should be – the sole criterion.

3 Looking for applicants

KNOWING ALL ABOUT the jobs that need to be filled or created and aware of the exact types of employee required, you can move ahead to look for people to apply for the vacancies. In accordance with your carefully developed personnel plan, you may wish to transfer or promote from within the organization. Alternatively, you might feel it would be more appropriate to recruit externally, from outside your existing workforce. Whatever you decide, you will subsequently have to choose the sources of recruitment you are going to use, and then advertise vacancies in an effective and cost-conscious manner.

Transferring and promoting Compiling your personnel plan will have enabled you to identify your current staffing levels, probable changes over the coming months and years, and future staffing levels; all set against a backdrop of actual staff requirements. At the same time, you should have recognized those employees who, perhaps after appropriate training and development, can be moved across or upwards into positions which become vacant or are established at regular intervals. If so, you need to contemplate the advantages and disadvantages of transfers and promotions, as well as the various sources of recruitment you can employ to tell members of staff about such vacancies.

The advantages Numerous advantages exist with internal recruitment. In particular, you know – or certainly should know – all about your employees: their conduct, work-rate, performance, strengths, weaknesses and so on. Thus, you ought to have a good idea whether or not the 'ideal person' is already employed by the firm, as and when a job vacancy arises. As time passes, you should be able to groom staff in anticipation of a forthcoming transfer or promotion, training and developing them *before* rather than *after* the move. Evidently, this all saves time and money when recruitment needs to take place.

Similarly, the chosen employee knows the organization well: its policies and procedures, the different departments and their teams, what to do, and – often as important – what not to do, and so forth. If he or she has been prepared for progression and is familiar with the new job, then it will be that much easier to adjust and settle into the position. Again, this saves the firm time, money *and* having to deal with the problems which often occur when someone takes over an unfamiliar job: low productivity, mistakes and friction between employees.

Often overlooked, recruiting from within the organization can motivate, not only the person who has moved across or upwards but colleagues and even the whole workforce too. They will feel wanted and valued, thinking that you turn automatically to them, as and when a vacancy arises. It should also encourage them to stay on in the firm, rather than look elsewhere for advancement, *and* to work harder and better than before so that they are moved upwards when further job opportunities arise in the future.

The disadvantages Not surprisingly, there are some disadvantages that need to be considered carefully too. More often than not, the next person in line for the job is transferred or promoted, typically because he or she is 'a hard worker', 'knows the job inside out' or – worst of all – 'deserves it'. No matter what the circumstances, the one and only reason why an employee should be recruited for a specific job must be because he or she is right for it, and matches the person specification as closely as possible. Otherwise, he or she will not be capable of doing the job properly, with possible knock-on effects on work-rate, performance and morale.

Even if you have groomed someone and he or she matches that person specification precisely, you should still open the post up to all employees who wish to apply, *and* go through a complete and absolutely genuine recruitment process. To just move an employee into another job without giving others the opportunity to put themselves forward will inevitably generate anger and resentment – towards you, the firm, and the transferred or promoted person. Clearly, it is sensible to consider others anyway: they may have hidden qualities which you had previously overlooked or ignored.

Perhaps the biggest drawback of internal recruitment is that the same people – with similar ideas, attitudes and approaches to work – are retained in the firm, and simply move into more senior positions. Those people recruited externally to fill the resulting gaps at lower levels will then acquire these (often dated and inward-looking) ideas, and so on. In an ever-changing marketplace (which you will have identified when composing that personnel plan) it is imperative that a company keeps up-to-date with developments, and this is more likely to occur if new blood comes into the firm in strategic positions, bringing fresh viewpoints with it.

Internal sources of recruitment   There are several ways of making sure that potential applicants know about a vacancy, most notably by issuing memos, placing notices on staff noticeboards and advertising it in the firm's newsletter, if appropriate. Memoranda can be sent to department heads to be read out at the next departmental meeting, or enclosed in employees' wage packets. This should ensure that anyone and everyone who could be interested in applying will be made aware of the post, *and* without incurring significant costs for the firm, although it may be time-consuming to photocopy and consequently place innumerable memos into wages envelopes.

Notices are an alternate or complementary method; and evidently, this is a cheap and relatively easy way of putting your message across. Nevertheless, it is vitally important that notices are placed on well-sited noticeboards, so that they are seen by the greatest possible number of potentially suitable employees. You may wish to put them in a staff rest area, by a vending machine, in the canteen or close to toilets assuming that both sexes have an equal chance of seeing them, to avoid accusations of discrimination. Just as significant, ensure that the noticeboards are kept up to date, with old notices removed regularly, otherwise staff will assume there is nothing new to look at, and will stop studying them.

Some larger companies publish in-house newsletters, magazines and journals for their employees, and you could advertise the vacancy in these, if appropriate. As with notices, this is a fairly inexpensive and straightforward method. However, there is a risk that it may not be seen by prospective applicants, or at least not soon enough. It all depends on the publication itself and how it is viewed by the workforce – if it is not circulated widely, is regarded as being dull and boring and is published only occasionally or irregularly, then the chances of this advertisement being studied are much reduced, or even eliminated.

Recruiting externally   Inevitably, external recruitment will have to take place at some stage – transferring and promoting from within may well be reliable, time- and cost-effective but the right person simply might not exist on a particular occasion. Even if he or she does, then a gap should eventually appear somewhere further down the line, unless your personnel plan indicated you should be reducing your workforce. Therefore, you need to consider the benefits and drawbacks of recruiting from outside your firm and – of some significance – think about the most common sources of recruitment available to you.

The benefits   The most obvious benefit of recruiting externally is that it enables you to bring new people into the firm, who perhaps have fresh and innovative thoughts, opinions and approaches.

All companies need to do this from time to time to make certain that they continue to keep pace with their rivals in the marketplace, and to expand successfully, as appropriate. Obviously, the recruitment of outsiders who are familiar with the most up-to-date theories and practices becomes essential if you are operating in a rapidly changing environment.

It could be argued on occasions that the installation of an external recruit into a key position will have a rejuvenating effect on those employees around him or her. The prospect of promotion is a factor in motivating staff, making them work harder, and strive to be better. However, if promotion becomes automatic with everyone moving up a position each time, then it is more likely to be taken for granted and is no longer going to motivate. Recruiting externally can thus make employees reappraise themselves, and try to improve their performance, now and in the future.

The drawbacks Without doubt, it is hard to recruit the right person from amongst a pool of external applicants – quite simply because you do not know them at all. To make matters worse, recruitment procedures do not always allow you to form a true impression of a person: letters of application may be written by a friend, a false image can be put across at an interview and a good reference could be supplied just to get rid of him or her as quickly as possible! Thus, the likelihood of picking someone who is partly or even wholly unsuitable is relatively high.

External recruitment is usually time-consuming, primarily because of the increased risks involved in employing an unknown person for what could well be an important job. You need to be as careful and as detailed in your approach as you can: creating well-designed advertisements, studying the various screening methods available and choosing the correct one in this instance, preparing thoroughly for interviews, and so forth. With transfers or promotions, some of these steps can be omitted, or at least compressed. For example, rather than screening interested employees, you may interview all of them.

Not surprisingly, recruiting externally will be costly too – certainly far more than transferring or promoting from within would be. Generally, internal sources of recruitment are free, whereas most external ones are expensive, and some almost prohibitively so. Printing and distributing application forms, acknowledging applications, inviting candidates for an interview and the like all cost money. To support your recruitment procedures, you may wish to test external candidates as well – either individually or in groups – and this is hugely expensive as specialists will need to be referred to, and brought in to conduct them, more often than not.

External sources of recruitment You can choose from a wide range of external sources. The most popular ones are word of mouth, notices, job centres, private employment agencies, schools, colleges and universities, the press and the radio. Word of mouth involves you and your staff telling everyone they know who seems suitable that a job is available, and inviting them to apply for it. This is quick, easy and free. However, it should not be used if your workforce is made up mainly or wholly of one particular sex or racial group, as it is likely that this will increase applications from similar people, and reduce them from others, which is unlawful. Also, it often leads to friends and relatives being employed, which is unwise: cliques form, members cover up for each other and you will find it difficult to discipline someone who has the support of everyone else.

Notices can be displayed on or close to the firm's premises, typically in a shop window or on a factory gate. These are simple and inexpensive to compose and put up and may be seen by people who are both interested and suitable for the job. As an example, young mothers would see an advertisement for part-time staff in a nursery store's window. Nevertheless, they can also be viewed by anyone passing by so thought has to be given to their contents and design so that only a small number of potentially ideal people apply, rather than everyone.

Job centres offer a free service locally, regionally and nationally as details can be circulated to others across the country. Staff can screen applicants for you, forwarding those who seem most appropriate, and allowing you to use their offices to interview if it is difficult for you to do so elsewhere. Nonetheless, only active job-seekers will apply if you use this source, and you may be seeking someone with current work experience. Furthermore, some job centres are notoriously poor at screening, sending along anyone who expresses a passing interest. Clearly, this wastes everybody's time and money.

Private agencies – which would encompass 'employment agencies' dealing with lower-level vacancies, 'recruitment agencies' handling managerial appointments and 'search consultants' who headhunt people for senior positions – perform a similar role to job centres. In their favour, they tend to specialize in key areas, maintain registers of would-be, suitable candidates, and can help with screening procedures. Against them, they are expensive, perhaps charging up to as much as thirty per cent of the annual salary on occasions.

Schools, colleges and universities have many advantages as a source of recruitment. You know exactly who your audience is, unlike some other sources, and can almost be guaranteed a regular supply of young people looking for temporary, part-time or their first full-time job, *and* at little or no expense. Of course, the quality and quantity of applicants will vary, sometimes enormously depending upon the educational establishment concerned, and how competent and committed teachers and lecturers are with regard to promoting vacancies.

The press – most often local or perhaps national newspapers – can be a popular choice. In general terms, it offers an extensive readership, publication on a known day possibly alongside other vacancies of a comparable nature and professional advice concerning the contents and design of advertisements. Nevertheless, there are disadvantages: many readers are not looking for work, those that are might not see your advertisement amongst many others, and the newspaper may be discarded after a day whereas other sources may be visible for much longer. Equally significant is the cost – typically running into hundreds of pounds for just one advertisement printed on only one day.

The radio is another popular source of recruitment. Your advertisements will be transmitted over a wide area, to many different types of people listening in, and a professional production service will be provided by the station to ensure that a polished image is presented – to job-seekers, competitors *and* potential customers. However, most advertisements are short and this makes it difficult to absorb information; also, few listeners are interested in advertisements and mentally switch off when these are on anyway. It is an expensive medium too – with each thirty-second advertisement costing perhaps £20 a time, and a dozen or more needing to be booked to have any impact at all.

Choosing sources of recruitment

Whether you decide to transfer or promote from within or recruit externally, it is essential that you pick the most appropriate sources of recruitment to use. Clearly, your over-riding concern must be that the ones selected enable you to contact the right types of prospective applicant, in the right numbers and – especially with regard to external sources – at the right price. Figure 3.1 (page 36) is a chart which highlights the different internal and external sources and these three, key criteria should help you to make the correct choices in your individual situation.

The right types

Initially, you have to make sure that your preferred sources will actually put you in contact with the right types; those would-be applicants who are as similar as possible to the ideal employee described in the person specification. However competent and thorough you are at composing application forms, studying applications and running interviews and tests, it is largely meaningless if you do not have the right types applying for the job – all it will do is to confirm that no one is suitable, and that you need to begin the recruitment process again.

The right numbers

Similarly, you want to be certain that you have a reasonable number of potentially suitable people applying for the job. Too few at this stage, and you will find that by the time you have progressed through the subsequent screening, interviewing and testing stages, hardly anyone will be left for you to choose from. Too many, and you will waste excessive time and money on sending out application forms, reading them, rejecting some, interviewing others and so on. What the 'right

Source	Types	Numbers	Price
Memoranda	Anyone interested – some good, others bad	More than required – but necessary to avoid claims of bias	Minimal
Internal notices	Anyone interested – right and wrong ones	More than needed – to keep everyone happy	Minimal
In-house publications	Anyone interested – satisfactory and unsatisfactory	More than necessary to please all comers	Minimal
Word of mouth	Friends and relatives – rarely the right types	Variable – often quite high and all expecting to succeed	Free of charge
External notices	Passers by – suitable and unsuitable ones	Potentially unlimited – according to location	Minimal
Job centres	Unemployed, mainly – some appropriate, others less so	Numerous – insist on rigorous screening	Free of charge
Private employment agencies	Often very suitable – depending on agency's register	Compact – if the agency is a competent one	Costly – typically 10–20 per cent of annual salary
Schools, colleges and universities	Youngsters – usually 16–21 years, of mixed quality	Plentiful – sometimes an endless supply	Free of charge
The press	Various – depends on particular publication	Extensive – according to publication	Expensive – perhaps £100 plus
The radio	Mixed – rather hit and miss	Extensive – but relatively few apply	Expensive – possible £100 or more

Figure 3.1: A chart highlighting sources of recruitment

number' is, must be open to debate although about twenty – assuming they are broadly the right types – is generally regarded as a satisfactory number.

The right price   The cost involved in using the different sources of recruitment has to be taken into account as well – it should be appropriate for the particular job and its role and value to the organization. You may be reluctant to spend much – if anything – on filling a part-time or temporary, lower-level job, whereas it could be worth paying hundreds or even thousands of pounds to recruit someone for a permanent, key position of strategic value. Any outlay also needs to be balanced against the source's ability to reach the right types and numbers of people in your individual circumstances. Be prepared to pay more if it attracts a sufficient quality and number of them.

Advertising   Having decided which sources are likely to reach the
vacancies   right types and numbers of people and at the right price, you can go on to advertise the vacancy through them. Your advertisements – whether in the form of a memo, notice, poster or whatever – must aim to encourage potentially suitable people to apply, whilst dissuading unsuitable ones who will waste your time and money. Thus, you need to contemplate the contents and style of effective recruitment advertisements, and think about judging the responses to see whether you picked the right sources, and advertised through them successfully.

The contents   The contents of your advertisements must be based mainly upon the respective job description and person specification, so that readers know exactly what is involved and precisely who is wanted; this will then enable them to decide whether or not your job is right for them and if they are suitable for that job. Hopefully, they will only apply if they can say 'Yes' to both of these unspoken questions. Obviously, the amount of information you include will depend on how much space is available: you will have to be much briefer on a card in a job centre noticeboard, for example, than on a poster in a shop window. Nevertheless, try to incorporate something about the company, the job title and its location, tasks, responsibilities and prospects, salary and fringe benefits, the person required and how to apply.

Typically, the company name and/or job title will head the advertisement, depending upon which is likely to appeal most to readers and persuade them to read on. Background data may then be given about the organization – activities, number of outlets and employees, expansion plans and so on. As with the job description, the job title must be absolutely clear and easy to understand. Unclear: and potentially suitable applicants will not read on whilst unsuitable ones may do and could subsequently apply. Give a specific location too. Some prospective applicants may not wish or be able to work at that particular place, so by stating it, you will limit the number of inappropriate applications.

Tasks, responsibilities and prospects can be taken from the job description, with only the most significant points being mentioned if space is limited. Try to provide as much detail as possible so that readers know what they would be expected to do. As important, be totally realistic, covering both attractive *and* unattractive aspects of the job – this way, those people who do not want to do the less pleasant tasks will simply not apply, rather than withdraw at a later stage when you may have wasted time and money on their application.

The salary and fringe benefits are key ingredients of successful advertisements, as they are probably two of the main reasons why people decide to apply, or not. It is wise to be very specific here, stating the exact salary or a minimum-to-maximum range, and setting out the particular benefits on offer to the successful applicant. Too many recruitment advertisers use vague and nonsensical phrases such as 'a first-class salary' or 'an excellent remunerative package'. Unfortunately, everyone defines these differently. Accordingly, a £20,000-per-year post advertised in this manner will attract applicants who believe the undisclosed but 'first-rate' salary is £10,000 or £30,000 per annum – with the first group likely to be unsuitable, and the second disinterested when they discover the truth.

Information about the type or person required can be obtained from that person specification. Include as many 'essentials', 'desirables' and 'contra-indicators' as possible; the more you put in, the easier it will be for readers to screen themselves, deciding whether or not they are the right person in this instance. Clearly, this saves you having to screen so many (unsatisfactory) applications later on. Should you be limited for space, then concentrate on the more important essentials and contra-indicators, rather than the desirable features which are of secondary importance here.

Round off recruitment advertisements by stating how applicants should apply, whether by application form, letter of application, letter with a curriculum vitae or by telephone. Also state precisely who and where they should apply to – it is surprising how many firms fail to specify this, and many, potentially ideal, applications go astray. Put in a closing date as well, perhaps for two or three weeks' time, as this creates a sense of urgency and encourages applications to be sent in *now,* rather than in dribs and drabs. A contents checklist for recruitment advertisements is shown as Figure 3.2.

The style Whether you are putting a notice up on your staff noticeboard or paying for a large advertisement in a national newspaper, you need to set out their contents in the best possible way, so that the right people are attracted to, become interested in, and consequently want and apply for the particular job. By and large, all recruitment advertisements should be eye-catching, brief, straightforward, non-humorous and non-discriminatory.

Whenever possible, recruitment advertisments should contain information about the following:		
The firm		
The job title		
The job location		
Tasks and responsibilities	– attractive	
	– unattractive	
Job prospects		
Salary and fringe benefits		
The person required	– essentials	
	– desirables	
	– contra-indicators	
How to apply		
Who to apply to		
Where to apply		
When to apply by		

Figure 3.2: *A checklist of the contents of recruitment advertisements*

First and foremost, your advertisements do have to be eye-catching – quite simply because the types of people you want to recruit may not necessarily study each and every notice or newspaper advertisement. Some will do no more than glance, browse or look half-heartedly, since they may not be actively job-hunting at the time: they may simply be curious and want to know what is happening in the jobs market. Nevertheless, they could be right for you, so catch their attention and make them read on.

There are many ways in which advertisements can be eye-catching; most obviously by being so large that they cannot possibly be overlooked. Alternatively – and most certainly far less expensive – you can choose an unusual shape, a thick border or a bold heading; perhaps the name of your well-known and respected company or the interesting job title. Also, you could use a logo, an illustration, different shades and styles of typeface,

Answering these questions should help you to decide if your recruitment advertisements are likely to be well designed, or not.

	Yes	No
Are they large?	❏	❏
Are they an unusual shape?	❏	❏
Do they have a thick border?	❏	❏
Do they have a bold heading?	❏	❏
Do they include a logo?	❏	❏
Do they incorporate an illustration?	❏	❏
Do they have different shades and styles of typeface?	❏	❏
Are they eye-catching?	❏	❏
Are short and concise words used?	❏	❏
Have jargon and technical phrases been avoided?	❏	❏
Are compact sentences and paragraphs used?	❏	❏
Have excessive, irrelevant and repetitive details been removed?	❏	❏
Are they brief?	❏	❏
Does each sentence make a specific point?	❏	❏
Does every paragraph cover one specific subject?	❏	❏
Are they logical and straightforward?	❏	❏
Are they non-humorous?	❏	❏
Are non-sexist words and phrases used?	❏	❏
Are applications invited from anyone who is suitable, regardless of sex, marital status, race, age or disability?	❏	❏
Are they non-discriminatory?	❏	❏
Are they well-designed advertisements?	❏	❏

Figure 3.3: *A questionnaire about designing recruitment advertisements*

or even colour if your budget stretches to this. You may possibly be restricted, to a certain degree, by your company's house style; nevertheless, do look around at other job advertisements to study different approaches, and decide which ones could work for you.

Be as brief as possible, so that readers are encouraged to go on to the end of the advertisement rather than lose interest and look at something else. To do this, use short and concise words which everyone can understand. Avoid jargon and technical phrases which confuse and mislead. Similarly, keep sentences and paragraphs as compact as you can, so that information can be absorbed easily. Be especially wary of excessive or irrelevant details, most notably repetition, as this can seem tedious. If in doubt, cut it out!

Linked to this, ensure that advertisements are set out in a logical, straightforward order: job title, location, tasks, responsibilities and so on. Each sentence must make a specific point. Each paragraph should cover one particular subject, and all in a clear and sensible sequence. Make certain that you avoid hopping from one topic to another and back again, as this is off-putting for readers who will soon become disinterested, and switch their attention elsewhere to another job advertisement.

Avoid trying to be humorous in your recruitment advertisements. Job-hunting is a serious issue – after all, many job seekers are unemployed and may have been for some considerable length of time, could have accumulated substantial debts and might be worried about losing their home. The job you are advertising – even if it is a part-time or temporary one – could be a lifeline for many applicants, and they will feel alienated and offended if you make light-hearted statements about it. Also, humour is such a personal and subjective matter; something which you find funny may be less amusing to others, or even be taken seriously by them.

Never discriminate in your advertisements, however unintentionally. Be especially careful with your wording: replace 'salesman' with 'salesperson' and 'he' or 'she' with 'the applicant' or 'he/she', even if this sounds clumsier. Less obviously, make it clear that you invite applications from both sexes or indeed anyone who is suitable by stating 'Secretary (male or female)' or 'We invite applications from qualified people regardless of sex, marital status, race, age or disability.' Figure 3.3 is a questionnaire which may assist you when designing advertisements, whilst Figure 3.4 (page 42) is an example of a successful recruitment advertisement.

Judging results   It is important that you appraise your recruitment advertising to see how effective, or ineffective, it is. Initially, you should compose a 'sources of recruitment analysis chart' similar to the one shown as Figure 3.5 (page 43). If you list the various sources used down one side and then note their costs and the number of applications received, unsuitable applicants and suitable applicants subsequently shortlisted for interview across the top, you can make comparisons between them. Typically, you can calculate the cost per applicant, in terms of the total, unsuitable and

Figure 3.4: A recruitment advertisement

suitable ones, simply by dividing the cost by the appropriate numbers. Obviously, more personal judgements need to made between 'free' and 'paid-for' sources; indeed, you may wish to draft two charts, as relevant.

It will take time to build up a complete and accurate picture of the success or failure of each source of recruitment. You will have to check each application as it is received to see where it came from. This can be done quite easily by including the question 'Where did you learn of this vacancy?' in application forms, and by asking it during telephone screening interviews. If applicants are expected to send in a letter and/or a curriculum vitae, a reference number could be put in advertisements to be quoted in the applications: a different number could be placed for each source. Later on, you will have to fill in the various columns as applications are sorted into 'suitable' and 'unsuitable' piles.

Over a period of time, during which numerous jobs will have been advertised, you should be able to calculate which sources are most appropriate for you, and perhaps even for certain types of jobs, applicants and

Source of recruitment	Cost incurred	Applications received	Cost per application	Unsuitable applicants	Cost per unsuitable applicant	Suitable applicants	Cost per Suitable applicant
1.							
2.							
3.							
4.							
5.							
6.							
7.							
8.							
9.							
10.							

Figure 3.5: A 'sources of recruitment analysis' chart

so on. From them, you will probably concentrate on using just one or two sources and can look more closely at your advertisements, compiling another form along the lines of the one in Figure 3.5. Different varieties of advertisement, with slightly amended sizes, headings, text and the like, can be set down one side with costs, applications received and so forth across the top. Again, you can then work out which variety of advertisement produces the best response and at the most cost-conscious price.

SUMMARY

1. To fill a vacancy, existing employees can be transferred or promoted from within the organization, in accordance with the personnel plan. Usually, the advantages of this outweigh the disadvantages. Vacancies can be advertised in various ways, most notably via memoranda, notices and staff newsletters.

2. Alternatively, people can be recruited externally, although any benefits associated with this are normally exceeded by the difficulties, time and costs involved. Vacancies may be promoted in numerous ways. The most common ones are word of mouth, notices, job centres, private employment agencies, schools, colleges and universities, the press and the radio.

3. To choose a suitable source of recruitment, it is advisable to judge each one according to whether or not it reaches the right types of people, in the right numbers, and at the right price.

4. Recruitment advertisements should be based upon the appropriate job description and person specification, contain as much relevant information as possible and be set out in an attractive and appealing manner. Responses should be evaluated to assess the effectiveness of the sources of recruitment and the advertisements themselves.

4 Shortlisting applicants

IF SUCCESSFUL, you will probably find that your advertisements persuade a fair number of people to apply for each job currently available. Evidently, you will not want to spend your valuable time and money on interviewing every single applicant, as there may be twenty, thirty or even many more of them. Therefore, it is sensible to screen applicants in some way, typically by application form, letter with or without a curriculum vitae, or telephone. You have to pick an appropriate screening method which will enable you to compose a shortlist of potentially ideal candidates to interview, and to reject the remaining, less suitable applicants.

Distributing application forms

The application form is by far the most popular screening method used today, and will certainly continue to be for the foreseeable future. However, its popularity does not necessarily mean that it is the right one for you as this all depends upon your individual circumstances. You need to contemplate its particular advantages and disadvantages *and* know how to devise one successfully. Then – and only then – will you be well placed to judge its suitability on this occasion.

Its advantages

There are some advantages in using the application form as a screening method, in comparison with the alternatives available. Detailed, background information about the organization and the job – a company report, sales literature, a job description and the like – can be sent out or handed over with it. Studying such documents will help a prospective applicant to decide whether or not this is the right type of job for him or her, and vice versa – if he or she is suitable for it. To all intents and purposes, it enables people to screen themselves into or out of the next stage, saving you the time, trouble and expense of having to do it for them.

Although each and every application form is – or should be – unique, most will include some or all of the following topics and questions, and often in this order.

Job applied for		
Where did you learn of this vacancy?		
Opening instructions	– Own handwriting?	
	– Block capitals?	
	– Black ink?	
Personal details	– Name	
	– Address	
	– Phone number	
	– Date of birth	
Education (from 11 years)	– Schools, colleges and universities	
	– Dates	
	– Subjects studied	
	– Exams taken	
	– Exam results	
Employment	– Employers' names and addresses	
	– Dates	
	– Job titles	
	– Tasks and responsibilities	
	– Salaries	
	– Reasons for leaving	
Leisure interests	– Hobbies	
	– Membership of societies	
	– Positions of responsibility	
Ambitions	– Explain why we should offer you this job	

	– Why do you want this job?	
	– Where do you want to be in five years?	
Other comments in support of the application		
Miscellaneous information	– Clean driving licence?	
	– Medical history?	
	– Criminal record?	
Referees	– Names	
	– Positions	
	– Addresses	
Closing details	– Statement that information given is correct	
	– Signature	
	– Date	
Interviewer's notes	– Comments	
	– Signature	
	– Date	

Figure 4.1: A checklist of the contents of application forms

If all applicants are answering identical questions in exactly the same order on an application form, then it will be relatively quick and easy for you to check whether or not essential and desirable requirements are met, contra-indicators exist, or whatever. For example, if possession of a full, clean driving licence is essential, you can turn immediately to the appropriate question, eliminating everyone who has given a negative answer. Clearly, some sections such as previous work experience will need to be studied more closely but even so it is still simple enough to compare and contrast applicants with the ideal, and indeed each other.

Its disadvantages The main disadvantage in most cases is that the questions raised are simply inappropriate for the job. Too often, a firm has one or perhaps two standard forms and automatically supplies these to would-be applicants as and when a vacancy arises. The forms are never tailored to the individual job and the questions which should be asked about it; therefore, school leavers try to answer numerous questions about

their work experience when they may have only ever had a Saturday job, whil
older applicants are expected to remember and detail their school activitie
from thirty years ago. Accordingly, they feel discouraged and perhaps aliena
ed from applying. Even if they do, you will have to look harder at th
application form to discover the information you are seeking.

Similarly, many forms are badly designed, with a youn
person's limited work experience having to be padded out to fill a huge box, c
a description of their personality crammed into a small one: again this is ver
off-putting for prospective applicants. Sometimes, firms seem to include ever
conceivable question that could possibly be raised, so that the applicatio
form is pages and pages long; again this can dissuade applicants from goin
any further in this instance.

Using an application form as a screening method i
both time-consuming and costly (assuming that it is done properly): it has t
be devised carefully in terms of questions, layout and style, needs to be print
ed, placed into envelopes with related materials about the firm and job, an
posted out. Clearly, this can be an expensive procedure, especially if you ar
having to deal with a large number of requests from interested people, both
suitable and unsuitable ones.

Devising an   Ideally, an individual application form will be drawn up
application form   for each job, or at the very least, a standardized form
                       would be amended for the occasion. This should not be
too difficult nowadays, if you have access to a computer or word processor.
Quite simply, your aim must be to ask the 'right' questions: those that give you
the answers you need, to assess whether or not applicants match the job
description and the person specification. Hence, questions have to be
absolutely relevant *and* easy for the applicants to understand. Figure 4.1
(pages 46 and 47) is a checklist of the topics and questions you could incorporate into an application form. You will need to pick out those which appear to
be most relevant to you, if you decide to use this method.

Consideration has to be given to the layout of the form
so that it is simple to complete, and the applicants do not have to squeeze
information into small spaces, expand details to fill large boxes or attach
sheets of paper which are so often mislaid. Have 'Yes/No' answers or squares
to tick, where appropriate; clearly, this persuades applicants to finish the form
as they can do so easily. Think about the amount of space that applicants will
require for each response; as suggested, school leavers and older applicants
will write more or less about school days and work experience, as relevant.
Always try to allow sufficient space, but no more. Excessive space discourages
suitable applicants who have put the relevant facts but feel they should have
added something else, and encourages unsuitable ones who waffle on end-
lessly.

The overall style of the form is important: it does have
to convey a user-friendly 'feel' if applicants are to be persuaded to fill it in. Do

ensure that it progresses in a logical manner – personal information, education, qualifications and training, work experience and so on – and avoids moving from one topic to another and back again, as some confusing forms do. Also, just ask the questions needed to screen in or out those applicants who meet the essential and desirable requirements and have none of the contra-indicators. Too many recruiters feel they have to impress by producing a form full of detailed, nitty-gritty questions. Accordingly, it runs to numerous pages and would-be applicants choose not to complete it. Remember, this is a screening method, *not* the final selection process. An example of an application form is shown as Figure 4.2 (pages 50 and 51).

Requesting letters   An alternative to using an application form as a screening method is to ask prospective applicants to send in a letter of application, outlining their skills, knowledge and experience, and explaining why they want and are suitable for the job. Alternatively, a covering letter can be submitted with a curriculum vitae which should contain similar information to the letter of application, albeit in a more structured format. Again, you should think about the benefits and drawbacks of this approach prior to reaching any decision concerning the best screening method for you.

The benefits   Being asked to supply a letter – with or without an accompanying curriculum vitae – can encourage people to apply because it is up to them what they state, how they phrase it and in which order. They do not have to puzzle over the meanings of questions in an application form, tackle irrelevant ones, fill out or compress their answers, or whatever; they have total control of and flexibility over their individual application.

Receiving letters of application and/or curricula vitae can be of benefit to you too, as it allows you to appraise applicants in a number of different ways. In particular, you can judge their initiative, creativity, writing style, ability to organize and present material, and the like. They can also save you time and money: you do not have to spend your valuable time composing a first-rate application form or spend your money on the printing, packaging and postage costs involved with distributing it to potential applicants.

The drawbacks   Unfortunately, one of the benefits of using this screening method can often be a drawback as well. Applicants are free to include or exclude whatever they want from their letter or curriculum vitae. As a consequence, they may not incorporate all of the information you want to check. If this happens, you do not know if it is by accident or on purpose. The details that are given will not be in any particular order, so you will have to study the letter closely to discover if your criteria are met, to

APPLICATION FOR EMPLOYMENT

Please complete this form in your own handwriting. Please use black ink.

Job applied for:

Where did you learn of the vacancy?

Name _____

Address _____

_____

Telephone _____ Date of birth _____

Education (from the age of 11 years)

Establishment	From	To	Subjects studied	Examinations taken	Examination results

Employment history (commencing with present or last employment)

Employer	From	To	Job title/ description	Leaving salary	Reason for leaving

Leisure interests (use this space to tell us about any hobbies, membership of clubs and societies, and positions of responsibility within them).

Ambitions (use this space to tell us why you want this job, why we should offer it to you, and any other comments which may be relevant to this application).

Have you ever been convicted of any offence before a court of law? Yes/No
If Yes, please give details:

Are you in good health? Yes/No
If No, please give details.

References (please provide details of two referees, including your current or last employer, if appropriate. Referees will not be approached until after an offer of employment has been made and permission to contact them has been given by you).

Name _____   Name _____
Position _____   Position _____
Address _____   Address _____
_____   _____
_____   _____

I confirm that, to the best of my knowledge, all information given is correct.

Signature   Date

Interviewer's notes

Signature   Date

Figure 4.2: An application form

compare this applicant's stated attributes with those of the others, and so on.

If the flexibility of a letter or curriculum vitae encourages people to write in, then logically it could increase the number of applications from both suitable *and* unsuitable applicants. Naturally, you will have tried to reduce this possibility by making your requirements very clear in your advertisements but there is always the risk that inappropriate applicants will still think it would be worth a 'quick letter' anyway. Overall, it could be argued that the benefits and drawbacks of letters and curricula vitae cancel each other out!

Handling telephone calls

The telephone is perhaps the least used of the screening methods available, although it might be the most suitable for you; as before, it depends on your specific situation. Once more, you have to consider the pluses and minuses of this particular approach *and* know how to manage incoming calls from interested applicants. Following this, you can probably reach a conclusion about which screening method is the one for you: application form, letter with or without curriculum vitae, or the telephone itself.

Its pluses

Talking on the telephone can be a fast screening method. You do not have to prepare application forms, send them out and wait for replies, study letters and curricula vitae, searching through them for the right information and so forth. You can have a list of key questions close at hand, ask them and obtain the answers that you need straight away. Conversations with evidently unsuitable applicants can be curtailed as swiftly as possible, with the best ones being invited in for an interview.

It is also the most flexible method available. You can ask a blunt, direct question such as 'Did you receive a 2:1 degree?' which demands a straight answer. Obviously, such a question could be 'accidentally' overlooked in an application form and ignored completely in a letter. Other questions can be phrased diplomatically: 'I wonder if you could tell me about …', or whatever. Subjects can be returned to later on if you are dissatisfied with the earlier answers, want further explanation or additional information.

Not surprisingly, speaking to someone on the telephone does allow you to appraise certain qualities that are hard or even impossible to measure by application form, letter or curriculum vitae. These include speech, the ability to hold a conversation, give sensible, logical answers, to be pleasant and humorous and so on. These may be key criteria for the particular job you are trying to fill.

The financial outlay incurred in screening by telephone is minimal, quite simply because applicants are paying for the phone calls, rather than your firm. This may not seem to be of major significance if you only have to deal with a vacancy now and then, but the savings in relation to using application forms will add up if you recruit on a regular, ongoing basis.

Its minuses   One of the biggest misuses of this approach is that it can sometimes reduce the number of suitable applicants who apply for the job. Some will be shy and nervous, perhaps rather reluctant to have to 'perform' on the telephone, especially if this is not a major feature of the job they are applying for. Other people might find it inconvenient to telephone during working hours, most notably those who are currently in employment somewhere else, perhaps at a rival firm.

At the same time, placing a telephone number in a job advertisement can increase the quantity of casual, half-interested – and therefore probably unsuitable – applicants ringing in. These people might not have the time or the inclination to write or call in for an application form or to draft out a letter or curriculum vitae, but may feel that it is worth picking up the phone and spending a few minutes chatting to you , 'just in case'.

Inevitably, using the telephone as a screening method will mean that you have to cope with an endless succession of telephone calls at all times of the day. Many of these will almost certainly be at very inconvenient moments, when you are trying to concentrate on filing a report, want to have your lunch or are about to go to a meeting. Clearly, this can be time-consuming for you or expensive if you bring someone else in to help out.

Rarely acknowledged as a potential minus is the possibility that you may be an inexperienced and/or incompetent telephone interviewer. With application forms, letters and curricula vitae, you can take your time, think things over and seek a second opinion if in doubt. On the telephone, you need to be ready with the right questions, asked in a sensible order, and phrased in the most appropriate manner. You have to be able to lead, control and conclude each conversation satisfactorily, both from your viewpoint and the applicant's too. This is difficult to do, and mistakes can lead to the right people being rejected, and the wrong ones interviewed.

Managing calls   If you are to screen successfully by telephone, it is absolutely vital that you compose a plan beforehand, listing the topics you wish to cover and the questions you need to ask in order to judge if the applicant fulfils your essential and desirable criteria, and has no contra-indicators at all. Too often, telephone interviewers attempt to tackle a conversation with little or no preparation. Clearly, this is foolish, as there is no chance that you will remember to ask everything that is needed to create a reasonably clear and accurate impression of the applicant. A checklist of topics and questions is shown as Figure 4.3 (pages 54 and 55), from which you can select those which seem to be most appropriate in your situation, assuming that you intend to screen in this way.

Even though each telephone interview will be different from every other one, they should all develop from the same plan, which may incorporate these topics and questions, in this order.

Initial comments	– Name	
	– Address	
	– Phone number	
	– Date of birth	
How did you find out about the job?		
The company	– Background	
	– Activities	
	– Goods and services	
	– Customers	
	– Competitors	
	– Marketplace	
	– Future plans	
The job	– Purpose	
	– Tasks and responsibilities	
	– Position	
	– Prospects	
Education (from 11 years)	– Schools, colleges and universities	
	– Dates	
	– Subjects studied	
	– Exams taken	
	– Exam results	

Employment	– Employers' names and addresses	
	– Dates	
	– Job titles	
	– Tasks and responsibilities	
	– Salaries	
	– Reasons for leaving	
Leisure interests	– Hobbies	
	– Membership of societies	
	– Positions of responsibility	
Ambitions	– Explain why we should offer you this job	
	– Why do you want this job?	
	– Where do you want to be in five years?	
Miscellaneous information	– Clean driving licence?	
	– Medical history?	
	– Criminal record?	
Referees	– Names	
	– Positions	
	– Addresses	
Any other questions	– The company	
	– The job	
	– Resulting from the interview	
Rounding up	– Thank you	
	– Will be in touch shortly	

Figure 4.3: *A checklist of the contents of a telephone interview plan*

Contemplate how the various questions should be phrased. 'Closed' questions such as 'Do you have three C-grade A-levels?' simply require a 'Yes' or 'No' answer. They can be used to check facts, keep a shy applicant talking, force an evasive one to give a straight response and bring a meandering applicant to the point. Avoid using them to excess though; nervous applicants will never develop their answers beyond 'Yes' or 'No' and a dull and painfully slow conversation will develop, and this will be your fault rather than the applicant's.

'Limited' questions begin with 'Who', 'Which', 'Where' and 'When'. As examples: 'Which organization ran that training course?' and 'When did you leave that firm?' Similar to the closed questions, they should produce clear and straightforward answers for much the same reasons, but need to be used sparingly to avoid a slow and sluggish talk. 'Open' questions starting with 'What', 'Why' and 'How' may sometimes be better. Such questions as 'What did you do on that course?' and 'Why did you resign from the company?' will reveal more about the applicant's personality, attitudes and opinions; or at least, will do so once the conversation has commenced, and the applicant is beginning to relax a little and feels able to chat more fully.

'Hypothetical' questions ask the applicant to put himself or herself into an imaginary situation, and to explain what he or she would do. Typically, these will be work-related if they are to be of any value. As an example: 'What would you say to a customer who demanded a refund for a product which had obviously been mistreated?' Evidently, they can be useful, but do be aware that the answers will indicate whether or not the applicant knows what should or should not be done in the circumstances. This does not necessarily mean that he or she will react in this way in practice!

Some questions should be avoided. 'Leading' ones like 'Do you have enough experience for this job?' are pointless because they tell the applicant what you want to hear and unless he or she is a complete fool, this is the answer you will be given. 'Multiple' questions simply roll several (potentially good) questions together. For example, 'What do you do in your free time?', 'Do you belong to any clubs?', 'What are your hobbies?' Not surprisingly, these will convey the image that you are rather confused, and will probably bewilder the applicant as well.

However they are phrased, 'discriminatory' questions must never be asked at all. Such questions as 'Could a woman do this job?', 'What will you do if your husband moves away?' and 'How will you mix with our white employees?' show that you are discriminating against the applicant on the basis of sex, marital status or race. This could lead to a claim of unlawful discrimination by you at an industrial tribunal, and deservedly so. Examples of closed, limited, open, hypothetical and leading, multiple and discriminatory questions to avoid, are shown as Figure 4.4.

Make certain that each and every conversation proceeds in a straightforward order: basic facts, education, qualifications and training, and so forth. Ask the questions, cover the particular topic and move

The following are examples of closed, limited, open and hypothetical questions, as well as leading, multiple and discriminatory ones to avoid.

Closed
Are you over 18?
Did you like your school/college/university?
Was your last job enjoyable?
Do you like sports?
Do you have a full, clean driving licence?

Limited
Who taught you that subject?
Which subject did you like most of all?
Where was your last job located?
When were you promoted to that position?
Why did you join that club?

Open
What did you gain from attending that school?
What did you learn from that work problem?
Why do you enjoy that hobby?
How would you describe yourself?
How do you see your career developing?

Hypothetical
What would you do if you failed your examinations?
How would you deal with an interfering boss?
How would you handle an employee who was continually late for work?
What would you do if that club closed down?
What would you do once you had progressed as far as you could within a company?

Leading (to avoid)
Do you have the qualifications we want?
Have you got the expertise needed to do this job properly?
Are you happy to work on your own as and when necessary?
Do you think your hobbies will help you to do this job well?
Are you ambitious enough for us?

Multiple (to avoid)
What exactly are these qualifications you have listed? Which is the examining body? Are they the equivalent of A-levels? If not, what are they equal to?
What was your last job? Did you enjoy it? What did you learn most from it?

Discriminatory (to avoid)
Are you planning to have a baby soon?
Will you want time off if your children are sick?
Do you think you could handle the white employees in the department without any problems?
Don't you think you are too old for this job?
Won't your disability stop you from doing the job properly?

Figure 4.4: A checklist of different types of questions

on; be careful not to go back over the areas, confirming the same answers time and again, in different ways. Also, concentrate on the key questions which have to be raised, to obtain the answers that allow you to compare and contrast the applicant with the person specification. Avoid talking at length; aim to have as short and concise a conversation as possible. You are screening, not making the final decision. Figure 4.5 (pages 60 and 61) is an example of a telephone interview plan form.

Picking a screening method   It is not easy to choose the right screening method, simply because the 'perfect' one does not exist – each has its own particular blend of pros and cons. Possibly the best way of selecting the most appropriate in your circumstances is to judge them according to what you want, what the applicants are likely to prefer and, not least, the time and costs involved.

Your wants   You need to consider exactly what – or more precisely who – it is you want, in terms of essential and desirable requirements, and contra-indicators too. Decide which method is going to help you most to appraise the specific mix, as quickly *and* as accurately as possible. More often than not, it will be fairly obvious which one should be picked in your situation: an administrative assistant will spend much of his or her time filling in forms, so an application form may be a sensible choice. Alternatively, you could be seeking to recruit a receptionist, which indicates that the telephone would be more appropriate.

Applicants' preferences   Take account of the types of people who will be applying for the job and their particular preference for or against the various methods. As an example, inexperienced and uncertain youngsters may feel happy with an application form – they can take it away, look at and mull it over *and* have the framework to work within. The telephone may scare them! As far as they are concerned, it is an opportunity for them to stutter and stumble, dry up and generally make a complete fool of themselves. They do not know what they might be asked – often a terrifying prospect at 17. Accordingly, some of them will decide not to apply, purely because of this.

At the other extreme, middle-ranking executives and above may feel restricted at being expected to fill in an application form, especially if it is a standardized one which has not been designed (or amended) specifically for the position. It does not give them the chance to explain, to amplify, to say 'Yes, but . . .'. It is all too cramped and limiting for them. They may prefer the telephone and the opportunities it offers them to talk, to detail, to answer queries and to win over the interviewer. They might simply be more familiar with it, and therefore more confident.

The time available   If you have drafted a personnel plan and are following
                            it closely, you should be able to prepare for recruit-
ment well in advance and can therefore pick the most appropriate method,
regardless of the time involved in using it. Nevertheless, there will inevitably
be occasions when you have to recruit as a matter of some urgency – a job holder dies unexpectedly and was in the middle of a major project which has to be
completed by a deadline, or a sudden surge of demand means output has to be
increased so extra staff must be taken on now. Thus, you may prefer to use the
faster screening method: probably the telephone. Whenever possible, you
should try to take your time – selecting an employee is an important decision
and should not be hurried.

The costs involved   It is sensible to bear in mind the costs of the different
                            screening methods when making your choice. Not sur-
prisingly, the application form is usually the most expensive, both in terms of
the time involved in its preparation and distribution and the associated financial outlay. Letters, curricula vitae and the telephone tend to be less costly.
Clearly, you do not necessarily want to spend substantial amounts of time and
money recruiting staff for temporary and/or low-level posts although you
should be prepared to invest more heavily to ensure that the right person is
selected for a key job, of long-term value to the firm.

      Composing   Whether you receive application forms, letters with or
   your shortlist   without curricula vitae or are telephoned by interested
                            applicants, you should set about composing your
shortlist of candidates to be interviewed in exactly the same way. You must
acknowledge all applications, assess them carefully, select candidates for
interview and then reject the remaining applicants in a pleasant and friendly
manner.

   Acknowledging   It is important that you acknowledge each and every
      applications   application as and when it is received (or follow a tele-
                          phone conversation with an acknowledgement of it).
Although this can be time-consuming and tedious – unless minimized by using
a standard, word processed letter – it does promote a polite and courteous
image of your firm. This will appeal to applicants and encourage their interest
in the job, *and* their continued association with the organization in other ways:
they may be customers too. Also, sending acknowledgements reduces the likelihood of applicants chasing you, which is even more time-consuming and
tedious. An example of a letter of acknowledgement is shown as Figure 4.6
page 62).

TELEPHONE INTERVIEW PLAN

Job applied for:

Date: Source of recruitment:

Name   _____

Address   _____

            _____

Telephone   _____ Date of birth _____

The company:

Background ❏   Activities ❏   Goods/services ❏   Customers ❏

The job:

Purpose ❏   Tasks/responsibilites ❏   Position ❏   Prospects ❏

Other ❏

Education

Establishment	Dates	Subjects studied	Examinations taken	Examination results

Employment

Employer	Dates	Job title/ description	Leaving salary	Reason for leaving

Leisure interests:		
Hobbies	*Membership of societies*	*Positions of responsibility*

Ambitions:		
Why should we give you this job?	*Why do you want this job?*	*Where do you want to be in five years?*

Miscellaneous information:		
Clean driving licence	*Medical history*	*Criminal record*

Referees:

Name _____   Name _____
Position _____   Position _____
Address _____   Address _____
_____   _____
_____   _____

Any other questions:

Comments:

Interviewer's name _____ Interviewer's signature _____

Figure 4.5: A telephone interview plan form

Dear

Thank you for your application for the post
of_____.

This is currently receiving our attention and we will be in
touch with you again shortly.

Yours sincerely

Figure 4.6: A letter acknowledging receipt of an application

Assessing The information given in the application forms, letters,
applications curricula vitae or your telephone notes must be compared and contrasted with the relevant job description
and – more importantly – the person specification. Ideally, you should be looking to shortlist the applicants who meet all of the essentials, most of the
desirables and have none of the contra-indicators whatsoever. Those who fulfil few or none of the essential and desirable requirements or who have any
contra-indicators will be eliminated straight away. A proportion of applicants
will be midway between the two extremes and you will need to use your dis-
cretion here. Although you will probably only want to interview about six to
eight people, it is sensible to see one or two more if in doubt, rather than risk
losing the right person.

Selecting Potentially ideal candidates should be invited for an
candidates interview, preferably at a mutually convenient date,
time and place (depending on circumstances). It is
essential that any interview is acceptable to both parties; this further enhances
the image of a friendly, caring firm, *and* it guarantees that the candidate will
attend. Too many (foolish) organizations set a date and time and then instruct
the candidate to turn up. Unfortunately, recruitment is a two-way process
these days and such an arrogant attitude often backfires. The candidate may

be unavailable then – perhaps away on an annual holiday booked months ago – and will not come. The firm may thus miss out on the ideal employee.

You may choose to telephone each candidate in sequence in order to arrange interviews; this is a nice gesture, being both friendly and informal. You might be working closely with them in the future, and it obviously helps if you can establish a warm rapport at an early stage. Also – and often overlooked – an unexpected, off-the-record call can give you an insight into their personality by the way they react, what they say, and so forth. If a telephone call is likely to be inconvenient and/or embarrassing – perhaps because they are currently employed elsewhere – then you should write to them instead, asking them to contact you so that an interview can be set up. Figure 4.7 is an example of such a letter.

During your conversation, you should not only agree on the date, time and location of the interview but also explain how long it will last, and who else will be involved; perhaps a personnel manager, department head and a specialist in the field. If relevant, ask him or her to bring in any verifying documents such as certificates and diplomas. It is surprising how many candidates lie about their qualifications and how few firms take the time to check on them. It is generous to offer to reimburse travel expenses for all candidates, especially if younger candidates and/or those who are unemployed

---

Dear

Thank you for your application for the post of _____.

I would like to meet you to discuss this position and ask you to telephone me on (01394) 727501 to arrange a meeting at a mutually convenient time and place.

I look forward to hearing from you.

Yours sincerely

Figure 4.7: *A letter inviting an applicant to contact a firm to arrange an interview*

are involved. Do this on their arrival at the firm though, when the expenses may be more realistic than afterwards when they are expecting to be turned down! Following your conversation, do confirm everything that has been discussed and agreed upon in writing; it is quite common for excited candidates to mishear your comments, forget minor ones, and to arrive at the wrong location and/or at the wrong time or even day! Send a letter of confirmation of the interview and also take the opportunity to include other material too. A map, with your premises and perhaps a nearby car park or railway station marked with a highlighter pen, is essential. Enclose some company literature and the job description as well, so that candidates can decide whether or not this opportunity is absolutely right for them. An example of a letter of confirmation is given as Figure 4.8.

Dear

Thank you for your application for the post of _____.

Further to our telephone conversation of _____,
I write to confirm you are invited to attend an interview at
(time) on (date) at (location). Any travelling expenses
incurred by you will be re-imbursed upon your arrival.

The interview will last for approximately ____ minutes.
Please note that you will be asked to provide evidence of
your qualifications during this interview. I attach a map on
which I have highlighted the location of our firm. I also
enclose some literature about our activities and the job
itself.

I look forward to meeting you,

Yours sincerely

Figure 4.8: A letter of confirmation of an interview

Rejecting applicants   Too many organizations do not notify unsuitable applicants that they have been rejected, simply because it is a time-consuming and potential costly exercise (although well-designed and carefully placed advertisements should have limited the number of applicants involved). This is unwise: applicants will waste more of your time by chasing you up, will be offended by your uncaring attitude and, consequently, will be less likely to re-apply for other jobs in the future, and for which they might be ideally suited. Also, they, and their family and friends, may be customers as well, and are not going to be encouraged to buy from such a hard-hearted firm again.

Therefore, always reject in writing, and as quickly and as pleasantly as possible. You should write a letter, as a telephone call raises hopes and then dashes them, and leaves you open to questions and a potential argument. Reject as soon as you can, so that applicants do not begin to build up false expectations, and/or try to contact you. Be as pleasant as you can be, but avoid stating a reason for your rejection as applicants may want to discuss this with you, and try to persuade you to reverse your decision. Keep rejected applicants' details on file for three months before disposing of them. This is the period of time during which a person can complain of unlawful discrimination to an industrial tribunal, so you need to retain records to verify your decisions, just in case. Figure 4.9 shows a letter of rejection.

```
Dear

Thank you for your application for the post of _____.

We have considered this application carefully but regret
to inform you that on this occasion you have not been suc-
cessful.

We would like to take this opportunity to thank you for
your interest and wish you every success for the future.


Yours sincerely
```

Figure 4.9: A letter rejecting an applicant

SUMMARY   **1.** The application form is the most popular screening method used today. Its advantages usually exceed its disadvantages, assuming that it is devised carefully in terms of its questions, layout and style.

2. Letters of application can be requested either alone or with a curriculum vitae, which sets out the same information albeit in a more structured format. The benefits and drawbacks of this approach tend to cancel each other out.

3. The telephone is the least used screening method, although its pluses can outweigh its minuses if calls are handled properly. A telephone interviewer needs to ask the right questions in a sensible order, and to phrase them in the most appropriate manner.

4. To pick a suitable screening method, it is wise to assess each one in relation to the recruiter's wants, the applicants' preferences and the time and costs involved on each occasion.

5. All applications should be acknowledged on receipt and assessed alongside the job description and person specification. Potentially ideal candidates should then be invited for an interview, with the remaining applicants being rejected in a pleasant and friendly manner.

5   Interviewing candidates

ONCE YOU HAVE COMPOSED your shortlist of candidates, you can move on to the interviewing stage of the recruitment and selection process. Interviews serve several purposes: they should help you to decide if the person in front of you is suitable for the job and your firm, as well as enabling the interviewee to conclude if this is the right opportunity for him or her; also, they give you the chance to promote a sensitive image for your organization. With these points in mind, you need to know how to prepare for, begin, direct and end interviews successfully.

Preparing for interviews

Your preparation for the selection interviews you are going to conduct can be separated out into a number of sequential activities: choosing the right type of interview to carry out, selecting the length and location of each of the interviews, and compiling an interview plan which provides you with a framework to work within. It is essential that these various activities are given equal attention as they *all* contribute to the subsequent success of the interviews.

Types of interview

As its name implies, a 'one-to-one' interview involves one interviewer and one interviewee. In its favour, it is usually relatively easy to agree a date, time and place to meet. If the interviewer is experienced and able, it should also be fairly relaxed and informal: a situation which will encourage the candidate to open up and talk more freely. However, the success of the interview depends largely upon the capabilities of the interviewer. If he or she is inexperienced, ill prepared and/or biased against certain types of interviewee, then it is highly unlikely that the right person will be chosen. Figure 5.1 is a questionnaire which may help you to decide if you are a good interviewer or not.

A 'panel' – or 'board' – interview comprises two or more interviewers facing each interviewee. Typically, the board would be made up of a personnel manager, department head, supervisor, a specialist in the particular work area, and trainee interviewers sitting in for experience. This

Being able to answer 'Yes' to these questions suggests that you have good, one-to-one interviewing skills. If not, there is room for improvement.

	Yes	Sometimes	No
Do you smile frequently?	❏	❏	❏
Do you look friendly and interested?	❏	❏	❏
Do you lean forwards towards the interviewee?	❏	❏	❏
Is eye contact maintained as much as possible?	❏	❏	❏
Do you avoid talking too much?	❏	❏	❏
Is the interviewee encouraged to express his or her views?	❏	❏	❏
Do you nod occasionally?	❏	❏	❏
Do you make encouraging noises?	❏	❏	❏
Do you listen carefully?	❏	❏	❏
Do you look as though you are listening?	❏	❏	❏
Do you add encouraging comments?	❏	❏	❏
Do you avoid anticipating answers?	❏	❏	❏
Do you avoid finishing sentences?	❏	❏	❏
Is the interviewee allowed to express his or her views?	❏	❏	❏
Do you go with the flow of the conversation?	❏	❏	❏
Do you interrupt only when necessary?	❏	❏	❏
Do you avoid expressing approval or disapproval?	❏	❏	❏
Do you hide your ideas, emotions and opinions?	❏	❏	❏
Do you ignore hunches?	❏	❏	❏
Do you maintain an open mind?	❏	❏	❏
Do you prefer facts to feelings?	❏	❏	❏
Do you reach a decision after the interview?	❏	❏	❏

Figure 5.1: A questionnaire about one-to-one interviewing skills

approach allows everyone to have a say in the choice, enables board members to share the workload and responsibility and to concentrate on their individual area of specialization: education, qualifications and training courses, work activities, or whatever. Not surprisingly, the broader range of skills, knowledge and experience available increases the prospects of the best person being selected.

Nonetheless, interviewing in this way does have some notable disadvantages too. Clearly, it is difficult to gather together all of the board members and the candidates at the same date, time and place. Using several key members of staff to interview is time-consuming and costly as well, and potentially damaging if it takes them away from other, equally important activities. Often, interviewers do not work together well, with some invariably trying to dominate, show off, score points and the like. Perhaps most worrying is that many interviewees find panel interviews to be very daunting, making them tense and ill at ease, and more likely to clam up as a result. Figure 5.2 (page 70) is a checklist of ways to improve a board's performance.

Length It is hard to know exactly how long to spend on interviewing each candidate: ideally, however long it takes to find out if he or she is right for you, and vice versa! As a very rough and ready rule, expect to allocate about thirty minutes for lower-level jobs such as trainee, clerical and secretarial ones, and up to sixty minutes and beyond for higher-ranking posts like sales representatives and department heads. More often than not, candidates for senior positions will face a series of interviews, with each focusing on a particular topic and/or with different interviewers, thus spending several hours attempting to secure a job.

Just as important when timetabling interviews – especially for those which are going to be conducted back-to-back one after the other – you need to schedule in sufficient breaks of about ten minutes between each of the interviews. Sometimes, interviews will simply overrun – the interviewee may have arrived late and could be rather talkative, or perhaps the interview was interrupted or you wanted to ask one or two extra questions. Even if you are experienced enough to keep them to schedule, you will still wish to have a few spare minutes to make notes, think things through, or have something to eat or drink.

Location The physical location of an interview can have a huge impact on the participants' ability to exchange information and discover all they want to know about each other. Whether you meet on the firm's premises or elsewhere such as a hotel lobby or restaurant – and hopefully it will be somewhere mutually convenient – it must be quiet so that you can both concentrate on asking and answering questions. Ensure you choose a place where there are no external noises to disturb you, like roadworks or heavy traffic. Similarly, make certain there are no internal distractions such as colleagues moving about, or hotel guests chatting and

Being on a panel of interviewers is notoriously difficult. Here are some guidelines for success.

Make sure everyone knows what they are doing and when, and agrees with it.	
Appoint a chairperson to lead the interview.	
Know what you have to say, and when.	
Listen carefully to other interviewers' questions and the answers.	
Never intervene, until asked by the chairperson if you wish to add any comments or questions.	
Steer clear of contradictory or argumentative comments.	
Avoid rephrasing earlier questions in a different way.	
Ask your questions when directed to by the chairperson.	
Use your one-to-one skills when it is your turn to speak.	
If other interviewers interject, ask them politely to wait until you have finished your questions. Look to the chairperson for support.	
Tell the chairperson when you have finished speaking.	
Make notes about the candidate's answers when the next interviewer is talking.	
Be prepared to play a full and active role in a panel interview; but without dominating.	
Give everyone your equal respect and attention; be as supportive as you can.	
Reach a decision after all of the interviews and by mutual agreement; it isn't always easy!	

Figure 5.2: *A checklist of panel interviewing skills*

laughing. Try to make sure you are not interrupted, perhaps telling colleagues not to approach you, turning off your pager, or whatever.

Think about the general layout of the interview area; generally speaking, do all you can to develop a relaxed and informal atmosphere as this encourages candidates to open up and talk more freely. Stand up, be still and simply gaze around the room to spot changes that need to be made. In particular, check that the sun will not be in people's eyes, replace a low and uncomfortable chair with a better one and perhaps sit in two easy chairs by a coffee table rather than either side of a desk. For a panel interview, sit around a circular table instead of on opposite sides of a rectangular one. Remove any distractions from the room as well, such as notices and calendars from the wall, and books, magazines and handwritten notes from a table or desk.

The interview plan   Each interview should be structured carefully and run according to a plan, albeit a loose and flexible one. Your plan should simply comprise a list of topics you wish to discuss, and questions you need to ask in order to find out if the person in the room with you is the right one for the job. Not only does it help you to compare candidates alongside your job description and person specification, but it assists you in other ways too. It acts as a checklist, enabling you to listen to answers without having to think over what you are going to ask next and as a reminder to move on when the conversation lulls, or meanders off in a different direction.

Not surprisingly, every interview plan is unique. More often than not, the topics covered will be those set out in the application form, letter or curriculum vitae, and in the same order. The questions should be linked closely with the points made in the job description and person specification, so that you can see how well matched each candidate is to the ideal, or not. An example of a typical plan – so far as one exists – is shown as Figure 5.3 (page 72). Whatever your plan, do make sure that it is an adaptable one, and that you are able to move forwards and backwards and add and deduct questions as appropriate.

Beginning an interview   The initial stages of an interview are a crucially important time as they will affect how the rest of the interview progresses and develops. Your overall aim must be to make sure that both you and the candidate are as well prepared and relaxed as possible and that – when you get together – you strike up a rapport as soon as you can. This should enable you to make the most of the interview.

You   Before it begins, check through the interview plan, job description and person specification to refresh your memory. Look again at the candidate's application form, curriculum vitae or your accumulated telephone notes. There may be a number of extra questions

INTERVIEW PLAN

Job applied for:

Date: Source of recruitment:

Introduction:	Interests:
1._____	1._____
2._____	2._____
3._____	3._____
4._____	4._____
5._____	5._____
The organization:	Ambitions:
1._____	1._____
2._____	2._____
3._____	3._____
4._____	4._____
5._____	5._____
The job:	Any other questions:
1._____	1._____
2._____	2._____
3._____	3._____
4._____	4._____
5._____	5._____
Education:	Conclusion:
1._____	1._____
2._____	2._____
3._____	3._____
4._____	4._____
5._____	5._____
Work experience:	Interviewer's name:
1._____	
2._____	
3._____	Interviewer's signature:
4._____	
5._____	

Figure 5.3: An interview plan

which you wish to add to your interview plan with regard to this particular person. Take these documents into the interview room with you, both for reference purposes and to jot down comments upon them, as and when appropriate. Try to relax, perhaps by shutting your eyes, switching off and taking deep breaths for several minutes. Be ready to meet this candidate; and remember, he or she is probably much more nervous than you are!

The candidate   Usually, the candidate will arrive early for the interview, so it is sensible to ask someone – typically a receptionist – to be ready to greet him or her on your behalf. If the candidate is ignored, he or she may become tense and edgy, and might even walk out. Make sure the candidate is acknowledged with a smile and that his or her name is known and used in the initial greeting, which sounds friendly and reassuring. Ideally, he or she should then be shown to a seat, have heavy coats and bags taken and put away safely and be offered company literature to read. It may also be wise to deal with travel expenses now, if these are being reimbursed.

Getting together   Of course, if interviews are well timed and run, you should be able to greet the candidate personally on his or her arrival. Nevertheless, if you are busy with another candidate, the receptionist should tell you that the next one is here at the earliest opportunity, perhaps within a few moments of the last candidate leaving. Do ensure that the interview begins punctually; if the candidate is left in the reception area for any length of time then he or she will become more and more nervous, and ill at ease. Once the agreed starting time has passed, that nervousness may turn to irritation and resentment as he or she starts to view you as inconsiderate and ill-mannered.

Always come out of the interview room to greet the candidate – if sent to find you, he or she may become lost and will consequently feel embarrassed and ill at ease when eventually meeting you. He or she might even disappear altogether; candidates have been known to panic at the last moment, and go home. As an alternative, the receptionist can bring the candidate to you, or a colleague can be sent along; either way, this is unwise. The receptionist should really stay in place to deal with other, early arriving candidates. Sending someone down creates a rather pompous, self-important image which you should be anxious to avoid.

Introduce yourself with a smile, a steady gaze and a warm welcome, such as 'Hello, Mr Munglani. I'm pleased to meet you. I'm Janet Wilson. We spoke on the phone last week. Would you like to come this way?' You may wish to accompany this with a handshake, although it depends on the individual situation; for example, the candidate may be holding documents in their right hand so proffering your hand may be awkward and potentially embarrassing. Make polite conversation en route to the interview room, perhaps about the weather or the candidate's journey. This can help them to relax.

When you arrive at the room, make a point of indicating where the candidate should sit down; this is not always obvious, especially in an informal setting. Think twice before offering a cup of tea or coffee; leaving him or her alone whilst you fetch it can increase tension, asking a colleague to do it leads to an unwanted interruption later on, and younger and nervous candidates will not be able to talk and drink at the same time. Similarly, be wary of handing over a sweet which he or she can choke on, splutter over or even spit out accidentally – it does happen, and is hugely embarrassing.

Instead, introduce your fellow board members if appropriate, and mention the topics that you (and your colleagues) will be covering in the interview, and roughly how long it will last. State that the candidate will be given the opportunity to ask questions towards the end, which you will be pleased to answer. Ask the candidate if you can make notes now and then, and subsequently do so in a low-key, discreet manner, so that it does not disrupt the flow of conversation; ideally when colleagues are talking or you are referring to your interview plan to see what you will be saying next.

It is important that you do not make any snap decisions about the candidate at this early stage, as so many inexperienced and biased interviewers are inclined to do. Each interviewee should be given a fair and equal interview, asked similar questions which are designed to allow you to compare them with the person specification, and be assessed on their ability to do the job, and nothing else. No decision should be reached until after *all* of the interviewees have been met.

Directing an interview

Once the interviewee has been seated and your introductory comments have been made, you should glance again at your interview plan, just to be sure what you are going to say, and in which order. If this is a panel interview, you will need to check when you will be speaking, and listening, as appropriate. Obviously, each and every plan is distinct although many will follow a similar, logical sequence of topics: the organization, the job, education, work experience, interests and ambitions.

The organization

The candidate sitting in front of, or next to, you will almost certainly still be rather tense and nervous, especially if he or she is young and inexperienced. This is a new and unfamiliar environment, you and your colleagues may seem rather daunting, and the job is one that he or she really wants. Thus, you should ease gently into the interview by talking about the organization: its background, activities, goods and services, customers, competitors, the marketplace and its plans, as relevant. This should be easy for you, and gives the interviewee a chance to absorb the atmosphere, become familiar with your approach, and relax more.

Whatever you say, concentrate on those aspects of the firm which will be of most relevance to the interviewee. Few will be particularly interested in its history, many will want to know about those activities which directly affect them, and everyone will wish to be told about its plans for the future. Try to be relatively brief and superficial – much of the information will have already been given, the interviewee may not necessarily be taking it all in, and you do wish to move on as soon as you can, when he or she seems to have relaxed as much as possible. Make sure your comments are fair and accurate as you do not wish to be accused of bias against any candidate.

The job Your talk about the company should lead on automatically to the job which needs to be filled, and you may decide to outline its purpose, tasks and responsibilities, how it fits into the organizational structure, and its likely prospects. Again, do be fairly concise and to the point about it; after all, details should have been supplied to the candidate prior to the interview, and your comments are just part of a general, easing-in process designed to prepare the candidate for various probing questions. Be certain that your statements are honest and realistic at all times.

Education Education, qualifications and training will often be discussed next: in detail with younger candidates who have not yet progressed to full-time employment, and in outline with older ones whose school, college and university days may be far behind them. Figure 5.4 contains a list of questions which should enable you to find out all you

---

Why did you decide to go to that school/college/university?

What did you most enjoy doing there?

What did you least enjoy doing there?

Why did you choose to study those subjects?

What did you like about them?

What did you dislike about them?

What qualifications do you have?

To what would you attribute your success?

To what would you attribute your failure?

How have you benefitted from your qualifications?

What did you think of your tutors?

Did you hold any positions of responsibility?

Why did you attend that training course?

What was good about it?

What was bad about it?

What were the trainers like?

What did you think of the other trainees?

What have you gained from that course?

Figure 5.4: A list of education questions

need to know to compare each interviewee with the person specification, not only in terms of education, qualifications and training but with regard to other aspects too, such as their personality, likes, dislikes and so forth.

It is sensible to use plenty of closed and limited questions here – beginning with 'Who', 'When', 'Where', and 'Which', for example – in order to check basic facts, force an evasive interviewee to give a straight answer, and persuade nervous candidates to keep talking. One or two open questions – starting with 'Why', 'How' and 'What', as examples – can be incorporated to give candidates the chance to develop their answers more fully. Make certain you ask to see proof of qualifications and attendance on training courses; many people embellish the truth, or simply lie.

Work experience   Each interviewee's work experience – and in particular the present or most recent job – must be discussed; briefly with younger candidates who may only have held an evening or summer job, but in considerable depth with older ones. A list of questions which can be asked is set out as Figure 5.5 and will help you to compare and contrast interviewees' experience with the work noted in the job description, and their personal qualities alongside those spelt out in the person specification.

What did your last job involve doing?

What were your main tasks and responsibilities?

Which tasks and responsibilities were easy?

Which ones were difficult to do?

What did you do in a typical day?

What did you most enjoy doing?

What did you least enjoy doing?

What problems did you have to deal with?

How did you handle them?

Did you work mainly on your own?

Did you work as part of a team?

Which did you prefer?

What did you think of your boss?

What were your colleagues like?

What did you like about the job?

What did you dislike about it?

Why did you leave?

Figure 5.5: A list of work experience questions

Closed and limited questions will reveal the facts about such matters as the job title, name of employers and lengths of employment. Open questions may be more appropriate though, to discover exactly what was involved, whether he or she liked or disliked the work, what his or her strengths and weaknesses are, the reasons for leaving, and so on. Switch back to a closed question – perhaps 'So, was the job interesting then?' – if or when an interviewee starts to talk to excess, or to meander off towards other, less relevant subjects.

Interests Leisure interests can reveal much about a candidate and his or her ability to do the job properly. For example, perhaps an involvement in amateur dramatics may suggest that the person is outgoing, and could be capable of making speeches, presentations, or whatever; this might be a key ingredient of the job you are seeking to fill. Figure 5.6 lists various questions with regard to this topic, and will allow you to gain a fuller understanding of an interviewee in relation to the job description, and person specification.

You can probably use a mix of closed, limited and open questions to find out all you need to know about interviewees' leisure interests. However, do bear in mind that most people are happy, if not enthusiastic, to talk about their hobbies and may wish to provide more information than you actually need. Accordingly, be prepared to cut them off with a fairly blunt closed question, or to move on to another subject as and when the opportunity arises. For example, 'That's great. Thanks for that. Now let's go on.'

Ambitions If you are recruiting in accordance with your personnel plan – as you must be – then you will be seeking to select someone not only for this job, but for future positions too. A list of questions is laid out as Figure 5.7 (page 78), which should enable you to decide if

---

What do you do in your spare time?

Do you have any hobbies?

Why do you like doing that?

What do you dislike about it?

How do you benefit from your hobbies?

Are you a member of any clubs or societies?

What does this involve?

What do you like about it?

What do you dislike about it?

What do you gain from membership?

Figure 5.6: A list of leisure interest questions

What can you offer us?

What are your strengths?

How do these suit this job?

What are your weaknesses?

How will you overcome them?

Why do you want this job?

What are your ambitions?

Where do you see yourself in five years?

Where will you be in ten years?

Figure 5.7: A list of ambition questions

Do you have the right qualifications for this job?

Will that training course help you to do the job properly?

Did your last job prepare you to do this one well?

Did you handle previous work problems successfully?

Are you capable of working alone as and when required?

Are you able to work as part of a team?

Did you have a good reason to leave your job?

Will your hobbies enable you to do this job better?

Are you the right person for the job?

Are you the ambitious type of person we are looking for?

Why did you choose that university? What subjects did you study? Which did you like and dislike?

What did your last job involve? What did you do in a typical day? Which tasks were easy, and which were difficult?

Do you have any hobbies, or belong to any clubs or societies? What do you gain from them?

Why do you want this job? Where do you see yourself in five or ten years' time?

Figure 5.8: A list of leading and multiple questions to avoid

the interviewee is ambitious enough to be transferred and promoted in due course, but not so ambitious that they will look elsewhere because you cannot provide the opportunities as and when they want them. Clearly, you do not wish to spend time and money on a person who is under- or over-ambitious, in relation to your particular circumstances.

Again, a blend of closed, limited and open questions should help you to find out all you need to know to compare each candidate with the person specification. It can also be useful to raise various hypothetical questions here, along the lines of 'What would you do if . . . ?' to enquire what the candidate would do in certain situations in the future. Of course, this does not necessarily mean that he or she will react as stated, but at least it will show if they know what should be done, ideally.

As with the telephone interview you may have carried out as part of the screening process, it is important that you avoid leading questions which effectively put the desired answers into candidates' mouths, multiple questions which simply confuse, and discriminatory questions which will offend, and leave you open to a complaint to an industrial tribunal. To help you to steer clear of them, some of the questions stated in Figures 5.4 to 5.7 are rephrased as leading and multiple questions in Figure 5.8 (page 78). Discriminatory questions that must never be used are listed in Figure 5.9 (page 80).

Ending an interview

Hopefully, you will cover all of the main topics and questions set out in your interview plan, and then find that you have five minutes or so of the interview left. It is tempting at this stage to conclude matters, especially if you are facing a series of interviews, and are perhaps behind schedule. However, you should use the remaining minutes to give the interviewee a chance to ask you questions and to answer them before rounding off the meeting in a friendly and efficient manner.

The interviewee's questions

It is sensible to draw your questioning to a close by saying something like, 'Well, I've covered everything I wanted to discuss. Do you have any questions?' The candidate's response to this will be revealing. An enthusiastic and committed person may ask you to expand upon various aspects of the company and job, filling in the background information given in promotional literature, and your earlier statements at the beginning of the interview. Questions about his or her exact role and responsibilities, training and development and future progression are all reassuring: the candidate is impressed by your firm and the job, and wants to impress you so that he or she is offered the position.

Of course, not all candidates will respond in such a positive manner. Some will ask a variety of 'What's in it for me?' questions about pay, fringe benefits, holidays and the like, which is understandable if you failed to detail or discuss them anywhere else, but rather worrying if such

Questions such as the following should not be asked because they indicate that you are discriminating on the grounds of sex, marital status, race, disability, age or sexual preferences. Hopefully you are a fair and open-minded interviewer and will not even have thought of them until now. If so, keep it that way!

How would a woman handle this job?

Can you manage men as well as women?

Do you suffer from any female ailments?

Are you able to work properly at 'that time of the month'?

Do you have to take time off with women's problems?

Are you pregnant?

Are you going to start a family soon?

How many children do you have?

How old are they?

What will you do if your children are ill?

Are you married?

Are you going to get married soon?

What does your husband do?

What will you do if your husband is transferred or promoted elsewhere?

How would a black person do this job?

How do you get along with white people?

Can you work with white colleagues?

Do you have any black customs or practices we should know about?

Will you want long holidays to go back to your own country?

How is a disabled person like you going to do this job?

Won't that disability prevent you from doing the job properly?

Will you have to take time off because of that disability?

Do you feel comfortable working next to able-bodied people?

Aren't you rather old for this type of job?

Won't your age make it harder for you to do this job well?

Are you gay?

How do you think our employees would react to working with a gay person?

What would our customers say if they thought a member of our staff was gay?

Figure 5.9: A list of discriminatory questions to avoid

information has already been put across. A few will ask irrelevant questions, perhaps about the time that the next bus is due to arrive, or the location of the nearest tube or railway station; again, this is hardly likely to inspire confidence that they are the keen candidate you are looking for. Others will have nothing to say, possibly because everything has been discussed, and hopefully they will state this. If not, it could be that they are not very interested in the job.

Your answers   If you have prepared thoroughly for the interview – by looking at company literature, the job description and so on – you should be able to answer any questions raised by the interviewee. It is important that your answers are always as balanced and as accurate as possible. Invariably, you will be tempted to give a more positive answer to a favoured candidate and a rather negative one to others, to encourage or discourage interest in the job, as appropriate. This is unwise; if the favoured candidate takes the job and discovers he or she was misled, then you will have to deal with a dissatisfied and aggrieved employee. Also, it is unfair as everyone should be treated honestly and equally throughout their interview.

Rounding off   Once the questions and answers have concluded, you should draw the interview to a close. Signal this by standing up, smiling and offering a handshake if this feels appropriate in the circumstances. Thank the candidate for attending and explain what happens next; typically, that you will contact him or her by the end of the week, or whatever. Avoid having to answer potentially awkward questions about the interviewee's performance or your likely decision, by moving towards the door and opening it. This should indicate the interview is well and truly over. Ideally, let the candidate leave the premises alone, or arrange for a colleague to show the way out; for you, the interview has finished. You have notes to write, other candidates to see and a decision to be made – but later on, after *all* of the interviews have been completed.

SUMMARY   **1.** To prepare properly for interviewing candidates, decisions need to be made about the types of interview to be conducted, their lengths and locations. An interview plan must be drawn up, which will vary from one candidate to another.

2. The aim at the beginning of an interview is to make sure that both the interviewer and the interviewees are as prepared and as relaxed as possible. A rapport should be established upon getting together and going into the interview room.

3. Each and every interview must follow a loose and flexible plan, typically covering the organization, the job, education, work experience, interests and ambitions. A mix of different types of question needs to be asked to obtain the necessary information.

4. To end an interview correctly, the candidate should be given the opportunity to ask questions which must be answered fully and accurately. It should be rounded off in a friendly but brisk manner, without indicating success or failure. Decisions are made later on, when all of the interviews have concluded.

6 Testing candidates

Using tests
Including individual tests
Incorporating group tests
Summary

FOR THE VAST MAJORITY of temporary, part-time and relatively low-level, full-time jobs, people will be transferred, promoted or recruited on the basis of an application form, interview and references as appropriate. Nevertheless, there are occasions when tests should be added to the selection process; most notably if certain, essential and desirable requirements are difficult to assess by these traditional methods and/or when the job is a key one, likely to play an important role in the success of the firm over the coming months and years. If relevant, you should know something about the significance of using tests and how to include individual and group tests in your procedures, when necessary.

Using tests   Too often, the idea of incorporating tests into the selection process is overlooked or even ignored completely; perhaps because they are an unknown quantity, sound daunting and expensive, and complicated to use. Whatever your perception of them may be, it is sensible to consider them rather more fully in relation to your current, specific situation with particular regard to their types, advantages and disadvantages.

Their types   Tests can be categorized under two broad headings: 'individual' and 'group' tests. Those which are set by individuals can be sub-divided further into 'personality', 'intelligence' and 'aptitude' tests. Personality tests help to compile a profile of someone's personality: attitudes, opinions, likes, dislikes and so on. Intelligence tests – also known as 'general aptitude' or 'mental ability' – test what is commonly called 'IQ', by looking at a person's verbal, non-verbal, numerical and spatial abilities. Aptitude – or 'special ability' tests – focus attention on people's more specific aptitudes such as mechanical reasoning and manual dexterity.

Group tests are increasingly popular nowadays, to the point where they are almost becoming an integral part of the selection process, particularly in larger companies seeking to recruit graduates for trainee management posts and for job hunters wanting to move into management positions. There are innumerable varieties of group tests, many of which are specific to an individual firm or industry. Nevertheless, most can be sub-divided into 'discussion' and 'problem-solving' tests. Discussions simply involve candidates sitting down and debating a subject while selectors watch and listen to them, and make notes. Problem-solving activities usually bring all of the prospective employees together to tackle a particular problem. Again, they are monitored and assessed throughout.

Their advantages   Tests, whether individual or group ones, offer several, key advantages. In particular, they allow you to appraise hard-to-measure qualities such as intelligence, personality and the ability to work as part of a team. After all, that application form may have been completed with the help of someone else, the candidate will be on his or her best behaviour at an interview, and an excellent reference may be given simply because the current employer wants that person to leave, for whatever reason. Clearly, tests, *if* chosen wisely and used properly, can provide a more accurate and reliable indicator of such qualities than your instincts are likely to do.

They can also act as a check on other attributes too. Bear in mind that your traditional application form–interview–reference procedure may have been flawed in some ways. Perhaps you were forced to use a standardized form because the firm would not invest in the production and distribution of an individualized one. Similarly, it might have been necessary to interview a candidate in an unexpectedly noisy environment where you both found it impossible to concentrate. By applying tests, you can have your own judgements confirmed or, if they were made in difficult conditions, re-evaluated, and perhaps amended.

Their disadvantages   The advantages of tests do need to be set alongside the disadvantages. Testing candidates is a highly specialized process; suppliers take many years to create and check tests for accuracy and reliability before making them available in the marketplace. A manager, however experienced, cannot devise one personally or pick a ready-made, 'off-the-shelf' test and just use it (even if he or she were allowed to do so by a supplier, which is most unlikely). Unless the test is well established and suited to particular needs, it will be of little use; the results will be unscientific and dubious and subject to personal interpretation rather than hard facts.

Tests are also costly to use: not only will you have to pay for reference manuals, test sheets, answer booklets and scoring charts but you will also need to attend a training course which will enable you to administer, score and interpret the particular test. You should expect to have to spend a four-figure sum, just to run *one* test. In addition, do not overlook the other, associated expenses – travelling to and from a course, work absences and the time taken up with actually running tests. An alternative would be to bring in experts to stage tests for you, but this can often be even more expensive. To decide if you need to use tests, simply look down your list of criteria and ask yourself a simple question: 'Can I assess each of these accurately by application form (or whatever), interview or references?'

Including Individual tests, which normally involve a candidate
individual tests sitting at a desk and completing a written paper, may
be set automatically at the end of every interview, or more likely later on as a separate stage of the selection process; perhaps for two or three outstanding candidates who really excelled at their interviews. If relevant to you, contemplate including personality, intelligence and/or aptitude tests, as well as where to go to obtain them.

Personality tests These tests are used more often than any others currently on the market, probably because all employers want to know whether the candidates have the temperament to do the job and will fit in, mixing well with existing employees in the department and firm. Typically, a series of statements are set out and a candidate has to mark one of the answers. For example, a statement might read 'I like to watch team games.' The range of possible answers could be 'Yes – Occasionally – No.' By answering a large number of questions in a short period of time – perhaps 400 in forty minutes – an accurate impression of the 'real' person can be built up, by comparing responses to those of various types of people. An extract from a personality test is shown as Figure 6.1 (page 86).

Intelligence tests IQ tests – to use the populist expression – assess the various aspects of a candidate's intelligence. Questions involving words measure his or her verbal ability and understanding of verbal concepts. As an example, a question might be 'Dustbin – rubbish . . . wardrobe – ?' The answer would be from: 'A: wood, B: clothes, C: furniture, D: bedroom, E: dress, F: cupboard.' Those questions using symbols test the candidate's non-verbal ability to differentiate between relevant and irrelevant data. For example, a star may be divided into twelve triangles with different shapes in eleven of them; the candidate has to pick one of six shapes to fit into the remaining triangle to complete the overall pattern. Examples of questions from verbal and non-verbal tests are shown as Figures 6.2 (page 87) and 6.3 (page 88) respectively.

Numerical ability can be evaluated by studying those answers with numbers, to see how well the candidate is with figures. A typical question here might be '3 – 6 – 12 – ? – 48 – 96 – 192' with the answer coming from 'A: 15, B: 18, C: 24, D: 27, E: 30, F: 36.' Spatial ability can be monitored by analyzing the candidate's responses to questions involving shapes. As an example, he or she may be asked to look at a flat pattern and imagine what it would look like if it were cut out and folded into a solid object. Figures 6.4

Answer the following questions by circling 'A' or 'B'. There are no right or wrong answers.

How would other people describe you?

    A   Rather shy.

    B   Not at all shy.

What kind of dreams do you have?

    A   Usually unpleasant.

    B   Almost always pleasant.

Do you daydream regularly?

    A   Yes.

    B   No.

Answer the following questions 'Yes' or 'No'. There are no right or wrong answers.

    Is your work interesting?

    Are you good at making excuses?

    Do you enjoy taking risks?

    Do you always tell the truth?

    Do authoritative people make you nervous?

    If you receive poor service, do you complain?

    Do you ever cry?

Give each statement a rating from 1 to 5 – 5 if the statement is always true down to 1 if it is never true.

    I am usually first in and last out of work.

    5   4   3   2   1

    I never put people under unfair pressure.

    5   4   3   2   1

    I make mistakes.

    5   4   3   2   1

    I keep my business and private lives separate

    5   4   3   2   1

Figure 6.1: Examples of personality test questions

Find the missing word:

Play _____ Work

(Answer: Ground)

Discover the word which does not belong to the group of five shown. Underline the odd one out:

Narrate

Recite

Compose

Relate

Declaim

(Answer: Compose)

Circle the correct spelling of these words:

Occasional

Occassional

Ocasional

Occasionel

(Answer: Occasional)

Underline the correct spelling of the plural of the word 'Stadium':

Stadiumes

Stadia

Stadii

Stadiums

(Answer: Stadia)

Read the following sentence, deleting any words spelt incorrectly. Place the correct spelling directly above them.

I am to busy to do it today

(Answer: too busy)

Figure 6.2: Examples of verbal ability test questions

Identify the matching symbols by circling the appropriate letter:

(Answer: B)

Identify the odd one out by underlining the appropriate letter:

(Answer: D)

Identify the symbol which continues the sequence by circling the letter below it:

(Answer: E)

Figure 6.3: *Examples of non-verbal ability test questions*

Do the following calculations without using a calculator:

$295 - 97 + 123 - 33 + 17 =$

(Answer: 305)

$18 \times 9 \div 3 =$

(Answer: 54)

$\frac{1}{3} + \frac{2}{3} + \frac{2}{9} =$

(Answer: $1\,{}^2\!/_9$)

Continue these series of numbers:

7, 12, 16, 19, 21, ____

(Answer: 22)

1, 4, 9, 16, 25, ____

(Answer: 36)

9, 6, 12, 9, 15, ____

(Answer: 12)

Figure 6.4: *Examples of numerical ability test questions*

Identify the shapes which fit together by circling the appropriate letter:

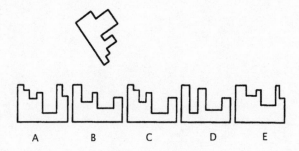

(Answer: C)

Identify the shapes which are the same by circling the appropriate letter:

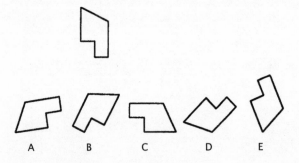

(Answer: A)

Figure 6.5: *Examples of spatial ability test questions*

Circle any differences in these lists of names:

1.	A. J. Bannen	1.	A. J. Bannen
2.	M. P. Hardcastle	2.	M. P. Hardcastle
3.	P. P. Kingsmere	3.	P. P. Kingmere
4.	F. L. Marvin	4.	F. L. Marven
5.	T. R. Quincy	5.	T. P. Quincy

Answer:

1.	A. J. Bannen	1.	A. J. Bannen
2.	M. P. Hardcastle	2.	M. P. Hardcastle
3.	P. P. Kingsmere	3.	P. P. King(mere)
4.	F. L. Marvin	4.	F. L. Mar(ven)
5.	T. R. Quincy	5.	(T. P.) Quincy

Find and correct any errors in the calculated totals. Put a line through any errors, writing the correct amounts next to them:

2 Chilli Con Carne	@	£4.95	£9.90
1 Lasagne	@	£4.50	£4.50
2 Mixed Grills	@	£3.75	£7.50
1 House Red	@	£6.95	£6.95
1 House White	@	£6.95	£8.95
3 Black Forest Gâteaux	@	£1.75	£4.25
1 Apple Pie	@	£1.50	£1.50
1 Chocolate Mousse	@	£1.99	£1.99
3 Coffees	@	£0.70	£2.80
2 Teas	@	£0.60	£1.20
Subtotal			£47.58
Service Charge @ 10%			£4.76
Total			**£52.34**

Answer:

2 Chilli Con Carne	@	£4.95	£9.90
1 Lasagne	@	£4.50	£4.50
2 Mixed Grills	@	£3.75	£7.50
1 House Red	@	£6.95	£6.95
1 House White	@	£6.95	~~£8.95~~ £6.95
3 Black Forest Gâteaux	@	£1.75	~~£4.25~~ £5.25
1 Apple Pie	@	£1.50	£1.50
1 Chocolate Mousse	@	£1.99	£1.99
3 Coffees	@	£0.70	~~£2.80~~ £2.10
2 Teas	@	£0.60	£1.20
Subtotal			~~£47.58~~ £47.84
Service Charge @ 10%			~~£4.76~~ £4.78
Total			~~£52.34~~ £52.62

Figure 6.6: Examples of special ability test questions

(page 89) and 6.5 (page 90) are examples of questions from numerical and spatial ability tests respectively. All in all, intelligence tests show whether candidates have the ability to reason, learn new information and think quickly.

Aptitude tests   These tests look more closely at a candidate's special talents in a whole range of areas. For example, he or she may be expected to read passages of text and spot differences, remedy spelling mistakes and grammatical errors or replace inappropriate words with more suitable ones. These tests check spelling and grammatical abilities, and the size and depth of vocabulary. Similarly, the candidate might have to study numerical information, recognizing alterations and amending incorrect additions, subtractions, or whatever. These measure cross-referencing and arithmetical abilities, in particular. Figure 6.6 (page 91) shows examples of questions from various special ability tests. Hundreds – if not thousands – of different abilities can be measured by using such tests.

Obtaining   To obtain personality, intelligence and/or aptitude
individual tests   tests, you will have to contact a reputable test supplier who will either train you to run tests yourself, or arrange to do it on your behalf. Whatever the approach, you do need to bring in specialist assistance at this stage. The British Psychological Society is the leading body in the field and will provide information, guidance and a list of individual test distributors, on request. They in turn will supply catalogues of their tests and will indicate what you need to do to purchase and use their tests in your selection process. See 'Useful contacts' on page 132 for addresses and telephone numbers. Figure 6.7 is an easy-to-read and use checklist which could help you to pick the right supplier and tests.

Incorporating   Sometimes, group tests are staged *before* interviews
group tests   are carried out, with all candidates being invited to participate perhaps during the morning, and then attend separate interviews in the afternoon. Alternatively, interviews may be conducted first, with only the top three or four candidates progressing to the tests which could be held on another day: it all depends on the individual firm. If appropriate, think about incorporating discussions and problem-solving activities, and be conscious of how to set them up, as relevant.

Discussions   It can be a good idea to seat candidates around a table – preferably a circular one so that no particular individual can dominate – and ask them to discuss a specific topic among themselves. It is sensible to give them a job- or industry-related topic, perhaps one which is especially up-to-date. Examples are listed as Figure 6.8 (page 94), some of which may be adapted to suit your circumstances. You and your colleagues can then observe, to assess each candidate's characteristics, whether

It is hard to know how to pick the correct tests and the right supplier. Following these guidelines may help you to succeed.	
Make certain that tests are absolutely necessary. Many attributes may be measured accurately in other, easier and less expensive ways.	
Be aware that tests are only one indicator of a person's skills, knowledge and expertise. They should not be used in isolation, nor be the decisive factor in your selection decision.	
Approach test suppliers who have been named by the British Psychological Society. Note that reputable suppliers only sell tests to those people who have the qualifications to administer and interpret them properly. Alternatively, they provide training.	
Pick tests which are of direct relevance to the attributes you wish to measure. Always use professionally designed tests, rather than home-made ones.	
Tests should be supported by clear and concise information about their purpose and rationale, the basis on which they were designed, the research carried out into them and how they were developed to their current, marketable status.	
Ensure tests are also supplied with a supporting manual which contains detailed statistical data to verify their validity and their reliability.	
Prepare candidates for tests by providing explanatory leaflets and/or practice questions in advance, or (preferably) by offering special preparatory sessions, supervised by the test supplier.	
Be conscious that candidates may be unfamiliar with testing procedures, and reasons. They might not perform as well as they could do, because of this.	
Make sure that test suppliers run the tests for you. Only those tests administered and interpreted by suitably qualified members of the Register of Chartered Psychologists will produce valid and reliable results.	
If you wish to run a particular test, obtain proper training beforehand from the appropriate test publisher or distributor. Note that this will only enable you to manage that one test, and no others.	
Give candidates some feedback on their test results, providing a printout of the results, an explanation of the scoring method and an understanding of its context within the selection process, as appropriate.	
Do not automatically use the same tests and supplier next time around – they may not be relevant on that occasion. Begin the procedure again.	

Figure 6.7: *A checklist for picking the right supplier of individual tests*

These are examples of group discussion exercises given to prospective police cadets. They are reproduced by kind permission of the Metropolitan Police.

- Do schools do enough to prepare students for 'the outside world'?

- Should drunk drivers be banned for life?

- Should the police be controlled by elected politicians?

- Should television sex and violence be censored?

- Would conscription cure teenage crime?

- 'You can tell what a person is like by his/her appearance.' – Discuss

- Is too much importance placed on qualifications?

- Riots: are baton rounds and water cannons the answer?

- Should charities be necessary in a civilized society?

- Is the Monarchy relevant in today's world?

- Unemployment: can anything be done?

- Euthanasia: the case for and against.

- Proportional representation: the case for and against.

- The smoking of cannabis should be legalized: the case for and against.

- Should smoking be banned in public places?

- Should animals be used for medical research?

- Bring back hanging: the case for and against.

Figure 6.8: *Examples of discussion topics*

- Working as a team, make a kite from the materials in the box – a black bin liner, string, and assorted sticks.

- A drum of dangerous chemicals has disappeared from within the factory. Working as a team, you must read the attached report and try to discover its whereabouts within the time limit set.

- Your group is in a hot-air balloon. It is overloaded. The group has to vote on who should be thrown out in order to keep the balloon aloft. Take it in turns to explain why you should not be thrown out without a parachute. Keep playing until only one person remains in the balloon.

- Working as a team, devise a computer program which will enable us to know when to re-order stationery items. Further details are provided on the accompanying fact sheet.

- The Chairwoman is due to announce tomorrow the closure of our factory in Westbury. Working together, produce a report advising her how to handle the press conference. Additional information is provided in the attached handout.

- Sales of our best-selling 'Duo' have fallen in the past quarter and the marketing director is thinking of revamping it. Working together, prepare a presentation advising him on what should be done. Further information is given in the accompanying handbook. Your presentation will be made at the end of the session.

Figure 6.9: Examples of problem-solving activities

they are a leader, team member, follower or whatever, and to judge how they mix with the people around them.

Problem-solving activities Similarly, the group could be given a problem which needs to be dealt with and resolved between themselves. Typically, they might be faced with a case study concerning an imaginary production, financial or marketing scenario for your firm, and be asked to consider and put forward proposals for approaching it. Each candidate may be expected to adopt a particular role, and to change places at set intervals. Figure 6.9 (page 95) sets out some possible problem-solving activities. As with discussions, candidates will be looked at, listened to and evaluated at all times.

Setting up group tests Although many firms attempt to set up and run their own, personally-devised group tests, it is far more sensible to bring in specialists to carry out what amount to complex, psychological assessments, or at least to advise you accordingly, before going any further. Again, you should contact the British Psychological Society and individual test distributors for assistance in this area. Refer to 'Useful contacts' on page 132 for contact addresses and numbers. Even though you may be handing over this stage of the selection process to a specialist, you will still want to be sure that you have made the right choices, and will wish to monitor proceedings. A checklist of do's and don'ts for you to follow is given as Figure 6.10.

SUMMARY

1. Tests should be added to the selection process as and when necessary, especially if key criteria are hard to assess in other ways or the job is of particular, long-term importance. However, testing is a specialized and costly procedure. Recruiters need to be trained, or must bring in experts to run tests for them.

2. Individual tests can be divided in three ways: personality, intelligence and aptitude tests. These need to be obtained from a reputable test supplier who will provide training, or conduct them, as appropriate.

3. Group tests can be separated into two categories: discussions and problem-solving activities. It is sensible to bring in specialists to carry out these tests, and to monitor and assess them in a professional manner.

Selecting suitable group tests and suppliers is a difficult task. Adhering to the following do's and don'ts may enable you to reach the right decisions.	
Do use discussions or problem-solving activities only if they allow you to assess otherwise hard-to-measure qualities.	
Don't rely on them too heavily though. Use them as part of the overall selection process.	
Do go to registered, chartered psychologists for ideas and training. The British Psychological Society will provide a list on request.	
Don't go it alone, running your own group tests. You may be best able to devise discussion topics and problem-solving activities but administering them and interpreting results properly requires professional knowledge and experience.	
Do pick discussion topics which are relevant to the job in question, and will enable all of the candidates to become involved.	
Don't select problem-solving activities which will not be experienced on a day-to-day basis. Make sure that everyone has the chance to contribute equally.	
Do tell candidates what they will face in advance, providing them with examples of similar group tests.	
Don't forget that some candidates will not have faced discussions or problem-solving activities before. You should make allowances for this.	
Do make certain that appropriately qualified psychologists sit on the assessment panel watching the candidates. Listen to their views.	
Don't overload candidates once the tests have concluded. The psychologist may suggest that some feedback is given, and in as positive a manner as possible.	
Do learn from the group testing activities – but do not necessarily employ them on a future occasion. Each and every recruitment situation is unique.	

Figure 6.10: *A checklist for selecting the right supplier of group tests*

7 Selecting employees

Appraising candidates
Making a job offer
Inducting employees
Summary

HAVING INTERVIEWED CANDIDATES and perhaps tested some or even all of them individually or in group situations, you should possess the information required to go on to select the ideal person for a particular job. To do this and complete the whole recruitment process successfully, you need to appraise candidates in order to reach the final decision, make a job offer to the right candidate whilst rejecting the others properly, and induct him or her into into the organization as swiftly and efficiently as possible.

Appraising candidates

It is important that a selection decision is not made until after each and every interview and test has been carried out, and you (and your colleagues, if appropriate) can sit down quietly and study all of the available information about the different candidates. You should be able to compare and contrast the facts, identify your first-choice candidate, recognize those who should be held in reserve in case your chosen one turns you down, and reject the remaining ones, as relevant.

Comparing and contrasting facts

Taking each of the candidates in turn, you need to compare and contrast the facts given in the initial application, your interview notes and test results with your requirements, as set out in the job description and, in particular, the person specification. To have reached the interviewing and testing stages, candidates will have had to have shown that they will be able to do the job and meet most if not almost all of the essential and desirable criteria, and have none of the contra-indicators. Thus, this should be a hard decision for you to make, albeit a good position for the firm to be in.

Identifying your first choice

Inevitably, it is never easy to select your first choice for the job in question; typically, some candidates will fulfil five or six of the eight requirements whilst others do the same, but for different ones. You may feel that one or two essentials are more significant than the rest; your colleagues could disagree. Probably, there will be relatively little to distinguish two or three of the six, eight candidates or whatever. If so, the deciding factor might be to evaluate the outstanding ones in relation to the personnel plan, and to ask yourself the question 'Which one is likely to be of the greatest, long-term value to the firm?' That person should be your choice.

Recognizing reserves Once you have picked your first-choice candidate, it is tempting to simply reject the others, almost automatically. This is unwise: he or she may turn down your offer if a better one has just been made or is expected. Alternatively, you might change your mind if you receive poor references or he or she fails a medical examination. Thus, you should keep your second and third choices in reserve until the job offer has been accepted and any conditions have been met. An example of what could best be described as a stalling letter is shown as Figure 7.1.

Rejecting the remaining candidates Whatever happens, there will be two or three candidates who do not perform well at the interview and testing stages, and do not appear to be suitable for this position. They can be rejected straight away, and in a pleasant and friendly manner. Do remember that you wish to convey a positive

---

Dear

Thank you for attending an interview for the post
of _____.

We are currently giving your application careful consideration and will be in touch with you again shortly.

Yours sincerely

Figure 7.1: A stalling letter issued to reserves after an interview

```
Dear

Thank you for attending an interview for the post
of _____.

We have given your application careful consideration but
regret to inform you that we are unable to offer this posi-
tion to you.

We are sorry if this is a disappointment but hope you will
be successful in finding a suitable position soon.


Yours sincerely
```

Figure 7.2: A letter rejecting a candidate

image of your firm. You might want them to apply for other jobs in the future (for which they might be ideally suited). Also, they and their family and friends could be customers, so you do not want to alienate them. Never give a reason for rejection as this can lead to further contact, and arguments. Retain details on file for three months in case a complaint is made to an industrial tribunal. Figure 7.2 is a letter of rejection.

Making a job offer

Not surprisingly, you will wish to offer the job to the best candidate as soon as you can; if he or she is that good, another firm might be around to recruit him or her. You can either telephone him or her or send a letter, depending on the particular circumstances. If the offer is conditional – typically subject to satisfactory references and perhaps a medical – you will need to deal with these matters promptly. Once the offer is accepted and conditions are met, you will have to reject your reserves.

Telephoning the first choice

If appropriate, it is sensible to telephone the successful candidate in order to make the offer at the earliest opportunity. Also, this gives you the chance to ask the permission to approach referees, make arrangements for a medical examination if relevant and discuss a starting date: probably in a week or two's time. However, it is easy to overlook key points during a telephone conversation, especially when talking to an excited person, so you should draw up a checklist to refer to, similar to the one shown in figure 7.3. Do think twice about making a telephone call though, only doing so if it is convenient and acceptable to the candidate, which is unlikely if he or she is currently employed elsewhere.

Sending a letter   Alternatively, or to substantiate that telephone call, you can send a written letter of employment to the winning candidate. This should set down the main details of the job: title, location, tasks and responsibilities, working hours, salary and the main terms of employment. Also, you should spell out any conditions of the job offer such as

A verbal job offer should contain information about the following:		
Job title		
Job location		
Job title of immediate superior		
Salary	– The amount	
	– Payment dates	
	– Payment methods	
	– Overtime rates	
Hours of work	– Per day	
	– Per week	
	– Lunch breaks	
Holidays		
Conditions	– Satisfactory references	
	– Medical examination	
Trial period (if appropriate)		
Time limit for acceptance/rejection		
Date of commencement		

Figure 7.3: A checklist for a verbal job offer

satisfactory references, a medical and an acceptable trial period of work as well as a request to accept or reject the offer within perhaps seven to fourteen days. You may wish to back up the letter with supporting documents, such as a job description and the company's staff handbook. An example of a written letter of employment is shown in Figure 7.4.

Obtaining references References should – but do not always – play a significant role in the selection process. They can help you check facts perhaps about previous work experience, confirm your opinions, possibly concerning the candidate's strengths and weaknesses and, most important of all, act as a brake, giving you the opportunity to pause, reflect and even re-evaluate your decision. Never forget that most recruitment procedures are fairly artificial – the candidate tries to create a good impression at the interview, and so on, and you may have been taken in by a smooth talker. A reference from a former employer, for example, may make you think again if he or she says that your chosen candidate can 'talk' but not 'do' a good job.

However do be wary of accepting references at face value. Personal references from family and friends are worthless; not surprisingly, they will simply praise the candidate, and avoid mentioning weaknesses. Be wary of accepting personal references from respected members of the community: more often than not these are from step-parents or divorced and remarried parents who have a different name from the candidate. Again, they may be biased. Educational references from tutors and headteachers may be used to verify qualifications and attendance on training courses, but little else. Teachers see hundreds of pupils every year and remember relatively few of them – except the best and the worst!

Current and former employers' references are most likely to be of value to you, as they dealt with the candidate day in and day out, and should be able to comment on how well he or she did the job and matches your person specification. Be slightly sceptical of what the present employer has to say though: it is far from unusual for a first-class reference to be given simply to offload an employee. He or she may no longer be needed by that organization. As likely, and more worrying, he or she could be a troublemaker.

Ideally, you should telephone rather than write to referees to discuss the candidate. They will be more honest and realistic, and feel able to make off-the-record comments knowing that these cannot be proven. Few referees – if any – will make derogatory statements in writing, in case these are seen by an angry candidate. As with all phone conversations, note down what you want to ask beforehand, to ensure that you cover everything. Use a checklist such as the one shown in Figure 7.5 (page 104). Also, write in advance, requesting a conversation, and outlining the exact areas of concern so that referees can prepare themselves (and only do this *after* you have had permission to approach them from the candidate). Figure 7.6 (page 105) is an example of such a letter.

Dear

Further to your recent interview, I am pleased to offer you
employment as a _____ based at _____. You will be responsible to _____.

The main tasks and responsibilities involved with the job are
listed in the attached job description. You should refer to this
before accepting the offer.

Your normal hours of work will be from _____ to _____,
totalling _____ per week. You will be entitled to a one-hour
lunch break which must be taken when convenient to _____.

Your starting salary will be _____ per annum, paid monthly in
arrears into your bank account. Overtime will be paid at
_____.

You will also be entitled to _____ days paid holiday per year,
plus statutory holidays. Our holiday year runs from _____
to _____.

Other terms and conditions of employment are detailed in the
accompanying staff handbook. You should read this carefully
before accepting the offer.

I would be grateful if you would confirm in writing within seven
days if you wish to accept this offer, and when you will be able
to commence work.

Finally, can you also confirm that I may approach your present
employers for reference purposes. Please note that this offer is
subject to the receipt of satisfactory references.

I look forward to hearing from you,

Yours sincerely

Figure 7.4: *A written offer of employment*

Sometimes, you will only be able to seek a reference by writing, either because it is your firm's policy or that of the organization you are approaching. Thus, you need to send a letter asking precise questions about the candidate's previous job title, tasks, responsibilities and pay, his or her attendance and time-keeping, conduct, honesty and abilities, health, length of employment and reason for leaving. Ask if he or she would be re-employed by that company; the answer will be especially revealing. Should you wish the referee to comment on the candidate's suitability for this job, send along the job description and person specification too. A letter requesting a reference – again, sent only after permission has been granted – is shown as Figure 7.7.

Arranging a medical examination   Good health is important in any job; clearly, you do not wish to employ people who are off sick regularly. In most instances, you will be satisfied that the candidate is fit and healthy enough to do the job by studying heath-related answers in an application form, meeting him or her at an inter-

A verbal reference request should include questions about these topics:	
Job title	
Tasks and responsibilities	
Pay	
Attendance	
Time-keeping	
Conduct	
Honesty	
Abilities	
Health	
Suitability for the new job	
Length of employment	
Reasons for leaving	
Wish to re-employ the person	

Figure 7.5: A checklist for a verbal reference request

Dear

Your name has been given to us as a referee by _____, who has applied for the post of _____ within our firm.

Accordingly, I would welcome the opportunity to discuss _____ with you, with particular regard to his/her:

    length of employment
    job title, tasks and responsibilities
    attendance and time-keeping
    conduct
    honesty
    abilities
    health
    reasons for leaving
    salary upon leaving

I hope you are agreeable to this. Assuming that you are, I will telephone you on _____ for your comments.

Thanking you in anticipation,

Yours sincerely

Figure 7.6: A letter requesting a verbal reference

view and talking to a former or current employer whilst taking up a reference. However, there may be occasions where a satisfactory medical examination is a condition of a job offer – perhaps when a job involves specific physical endeavour or the post is a key one of long-term, strategic significance, and you cannot afford to have any absences at all.

If you work for a larger firm, you may have your own medical team on site who can arrange for an appropriate check-up to take place, at a mutually convenient time. Alternatively, your organization might have set up medical insurance cover for the workforce, perhaps through a private heath insurance company such as BUPA or PPP. Accordingly, it may be possible to book a medical examination for the candidate at one of their centres across the country. Naturally, you should pay for this, along with any reasonable travel expenses incurred. Addresses and telephone numbers for BUPA and PPP are listed under 'Useful contacts' on page 132.

Should you be employed by or perhaps own a smaller concern, you could arrange for a medical check-up to be carried out by the candidate's own doctor, with the business covering the cost of this and any associated expenses paid out by the candidate in relation to it. Under the terms of the Access to Medical Reports Act 1988, you need to have the consent of a

```
Dear

Your name has been given to us as a referee by _____ , who has
applied for the post of _____ within our firm.

As such, we would be grateful if you could answer the following
questions. All information supplied will be treated in the stri-
cest confidence.

    How long was he/she employed by you?
    What was his/her job title?
    What did this job involve doing?
    How would you relate him/her in relation to (a) attendance
    and time-keeping, (b) conduct, (c) honesty, (d) ability to
    do the job, (e) health?
    What was his/her reason for leaving?
    What was his/her salary upon leaving?
    Would you re-employ him/her?

A stamped addressed envelope is enclosed. Thank you for your
assistance.


Yours sincerely
```

Figure 7.7: A letter requesting a written reference

person to your application for medical information about him or her from the doctor – so this must be obtained beforehand in writing and forwarded to the doctor with your request, in due course.

Rejecting the reserves As soon as your chosen candidate has accepted your offer and any conditions have been met, you should reject the second- and third-placed candidates whom you have been holding in reserve, just in case. Once more, you wish to put across a warm and caring image to these potential customers and prospective future applicants for other posts that become vacant. Send a pleasant but vague letter without actually stating a reason for the rejection, which could lead on to disputes and disagreements. File away candidates' details for three months in case you need to prove that you treated everyone fairly at an industrial tribunal. Refer again to Figure 7.2 as an example of a letter of rejection.

Inducting employees Recruitment does not – or certainly should not – come to an abrupt end once the candidate has been chosen and agreed to join your organization. To be considered successful, you need to make sure each and every recruit, whether transferred or promoted, or recruited externally, is settled into a new job as quickly and smoothly as possible, so that work-rate, performance and team work are maximized at the earliest possible opportunity. Induction – as this process is commonly known – can be divided into three stages. It should really begin during recruitment, continue with a special induction day and be completed in the early weeks of starting work. If the recruit has been taken on for a trial period, you should then be able to confirm his or her employment.

During recruitment In order to settle someone into a new position swiftly and efficiently, he or she needs to get to know the job and the firm inside out, and you and your colleagues have to understand him or her equally well. Your recruitment and selection procedures have been designed to do just this: sending out job descriptions and company literature with application forms, talking about the job, organization and the recruit in interviews and so forth. The more you both know, the easier it will be for the recruit to settle down and start contributing to the organization.

The induction day Once the job offer has been accepted and any conditions fulfilled, it is sensible to invite the recruit to spend a half or full day with the organization before he or she starts work properly. This is an opportunity for everyone to find out more about each other, and to identify and deal with any obvious shortcomings, misunderstandings, worries and queries. Obviously, each and every induction day programme will vary according to individual circumstances, although they should all have certain, basic activities in common. Figure 7.8 contains a 'typical' induction day schedule, so far as one exists.

As with the selection interview, come and greet the recruit in person, on his or her arrival if possible, to show you are a concerned and caring employer. Perhaps start the day by guiding the recruit around all of the premises so that he or she can gain a better understanding of what is happening, and where. You should in particular point out everything of key concern to the recruit: his or her own department, work area, immediate supervisor and colleagues, frequently or occasionally used areas and other employees with whom he or she will be in occasional and/or regular contact. Always indicate where the toilets, restrooms, canteen and restaurant facilities are; invariably, these are of interest to everybody.

Then take a break, having a tea or coffee whilst chatting about the organization and the job in more depth. Work through company literature, the job description, the terms and conditions of employment, the staff handbook to confirm facts and fill in any gaps. Take time to discover whether the recruit has any concerns or questions about any aspects of his or her forthcoming employment. Deal with any administrative details at this stage too, possibly making a note of his or her bank account and national insurance number for wages purposes, and receiving a P45 from the last employer, if relevant. Should these not be readily available, ask the recruit to bring them in on his or her first day of work.

Up to lunchtime, it may be a good idea to take him or her back to the department where the job will be carried out. Spend some time introducing the recruit to the immediate superior and each of his or her colleagues in turn, allowing them to chat together about their respective work loads, how they will liaise and co-operate with each other and so on. Try to ensure that he or she meets and speaks to everyone to everyone of significance to the particular job. Encourage the recruit to have lunch with the immediate superior or more likely a new colleague to increase his or her knowledge and build up a rapport. Preferably, this should be a keen and hardworking employee so that his or her attributes rub off on the recruit!

After lunch, let the recruit sit in the department and watch what is going on. If the departing job-holder is available, it is sensible to put them together at this time, but only if he or she is an agreeable person who has a high opinion of the job and the firm. If not, a close and trustworthy colleague should act as a minder instead. As the afternoon progresses, the recruit may be encouraged to attempt certain tasks, particularly new ones, under the careful supervision of the colleague. Hopefully, this will build confidence for when he or she begins work properly.

At the end of the induction day, you should come back and see the recruit, chatting to him or her, the immediate superior and the minder, to make sure all is well and any queries can be cleared up. Remind the recruit that he or she needs to bring in certain items on the first day; typically bank account details and the national insurance number so that he or she can

INDUCTION DAY TIMETABLE

9.30	**Greet recruit on arrival:**	in person.
9.30 – 10.45	**Tour of premises:**	department
		work area
		immediate superior
		colleagues
		frequently used areas
		occasionally used areas
		other employees
		toilets
		restrooms
		canteens
		restaurant facilities
		others?
10.45 – 11.30	**Coffee break and talk:**	company
		job
		terms and conditions of employment
		staff handbook
		administrative details
		queries?
11.30 – 1.00	**Tour of department:**	immediate superior
		colleagues
		work area
		workload
1.00 – 2.15	**Lunch:**	with a keen, hardworking employee
2.15 – 3.30	**Watching job activities:**	sitting alongside the departing job holder or a trusted 'minder'.
3.30 – 3.50	**Tea break:**	check that all is well.
3.50 – 4.50	**Attempting job activities:**	under the supervision of the departing job holder or the trusted minder.
4.50 – 5.00	**Farewell conversation:**	with immediate superior and minder.
		queries?
		items to bring in on first day
		will be paid for today
		smile, handshake, wave.

Figure 7.8: An induction day programme

be paid on time. Thank him or her for coming in and perhaps say he or she will be paid for the time, which is a nice touch and creates a fair and decent image of your concern. Make it clear that you are looking forward to him or her join- ing the team, and are always there to help if needed. Show the recruit out with a warm smile, handshake and a cheery wave.

The early weeks   Make certain that everything is prepared for the recruit's arrival on their first day at work: a desk is emp- tied, a locker is cleared out, a uniform is available, or whatever. Similarly, be sure that everyone knows he or she is starting on that day and is ready to wel- come them with a smile, helpful comments and the like. Meet the recruit personally as you did on the induction day, before passing him or her over to the immediate superior and the minder, who will keep a watchful eye out, give guidance and tackle any problems. Check that all is well with the recruit at break times, lunch and at the end of the day. Be 'around' at all times in case dif- ficulties arise which only you can resolve.

During the first week, you should make a point of see- ing and talking to the recruit at least once each day to check developments, deal with any problems and eliminate worries. Speak to the immediate superi- or and the minder too, in order to ensure that he or she is working well. Generally make yourself accessible so that he or she can approach you, if nec- essary. Hopefully, as the week progresses, you will feel able to become less visible although it is important that the recruit knows you are available, if or when required.

After one month, it is wise to assess the recruit's work to date. Chat informally about the job, work-rate and performance, likes, dis- likes, strengths, weaknesses and any problems that exist. You may wish to base this discussion around the checklist of points shown in Figure 7.9. Then talk to the immediate superior and perhaps the minder to obtain their views about the recruit. Hopefully, any difficulties – which will usually develop from inexperi- ence and uncertainty if you have chosen the right person – will be minor ones and can be remedied with a little care and attention.

Confirming   Often, a recruit will be taken on for a trial period, with
employment   employment being confirmed once he or she has set- tled into the job. A letter of confirmation will then be sent, like the one shown in Figure 7.10 (page 112). In accordance with the Employment Protection (Consolidation) Act 1978, a written statement of the main terms of employment has to be given to employees who work more than sixteen hours or more each week, within thirteen weeks of starting work. This should detail the employer's and employee's names, the date of commence- ment, the job title, hours of work, rate and frequency of pay, holiday and sickness pay and arrangements, disciplinary, grievance, appeal and notice rules and procedures, and pension entitlements. This, and supporting docu- ments such as a staff handbook, will normally accompany the letter of

Discussing the following topics should ensure that a complete and thorough work review takes place.	
Attendance	
Time-keeping	
Personal appearance	
General conduct	
Work-rate	
Work performance	
Work relations	
Likes	
Dislikes	
Strengths	
Weaknesses	
Problems	
Recommendation for improvements	

Figure 7.9: A checklist of points to be raised during a work review

confirmation. An example of a written statement is given in Figure 7.11 (page 113).

SUMMARY 1. A selection decision must not be made until after each and every interview and test has been carried out. All accumulated information can then be compared to and contrasted with requirements. A first-choice candidate should be identified with two or three others kept in reserve just in case. Remaining candidates can consequently be rejected, in a polite and friendly manner.

2. A job offer may be made by telephone or by letter. It is sensible to make it conditional, typically upon receipt of satisfactory references and perhaps a

Dear

I am pleased to be able to confirm your employment as _____
following the successful completion of your trial period.

I enclose two copies of your written statement of the main terms
and conditions of employment. Please sign both, returning one to
me and retaining the other for your future reference.

I am delighted to welcome you to _____ and hope you will
have a long and rewarding career with us.

With good wishes,

Yours sincerely

Figure 7.10: A letter confirming employment

medical examination. Once the offer has been accepted and conditions have been met, the reserves can be rejected, as pleasantly as possible.

3. A recruit should be inducted into a new job quickly and smoothly. This process begins during recruitment, continues with a special, one-day induction programme and progresses through the early weeks. As soon as he or she has settled in and is doing well, permanent employment will usually be confirmed.

STATEMENT OF EMPLOYMENT

Employer _____

Employee _____

Your employment commenced on _____

You are employed as _____

The job is located at _____

Your normal hours of work are _____

Your pay is _____

Your method of payment is _____

Overtime is paid at the rate of _____

You are entitled to _____ days paid holiday plus paid statutory holidays each year. Our holiday year runs from _____ to _____.

Disciplinary, grievance and appeal rules and procedures are detailed in the staff handbook supplied with this written statement.

Sickness pay and arrangements and the company's pension scheme are also detailed in the staff handbook. A copy is available in the staff restroom for inspection at any time.

Notice to be given by the employer is _____

Notice to be given by the employee is _____

Employer's signature _____

Date _____

Employee's signature _____

Date _____

Figure 7.11: A written statement of the main terms and conditions of employment

8 Developing a personnel plan

Evaluating staff needs
Monitoring staffing levels
Maintaining the plan
Summary

WITHOUT DOUBT, recruitment is the major ingredient in an effective personnel plan as you bring in, transfer across or move up the right types and numbers of people into the right places and at the right times; all to match staff needs and levels as closely as possible. Nevertheless, that plan does have to be developed on an ongoing basis and amended as appropriate, if it is to continue to be useable. Thus, you should constantly evaluate staff needs, monitoring staff levels and generally maintain the plan so that it remains effective both now and in the long term.

Evaluating staff needs   Clearly, you will have been aware of your existing staff needs when the plan was introduced, identified the likely internal and external influences upon them and analyzed your future staffing needs too; and will have subsequently been working towards them. However, you do need to keep a close, ever-watchful eye on those internal and external factors to make certain that they develop as expected rather than changing unexpectedly, as this would affect your staffing requirements in the future, and perhaps quite dramatically.

Internal factors   If you are to build up and maintain this personnel plan, you should adopt and follow the motto 'Think ahead', making sure that you are continually looking at what is happening today and working out how it will affect the quality and quantity of staff required tomorrow. Thus, be sure to stay up-to-date with company literature: memoranda, newsletters, reports, projections, proposals and the like. Try to be conscious of the company's organizational, business and trading plans for the future, and how these might influence your requirements. Figure 8.1 is a questionnaire which may help you to ascertain if you are up-to-date.

External factors   Likewise, you must be familiar with all the external factors which could potentially have an impact on the types and numbers of employee needed by your firm – and know what is

If you can say 'Yes' to these questions, you are probably up to date with most if not almost all of the internal factors which affect your staff requirements.

	Yes	No
Do you know exactly what your organization's policies are at the moment?	❑	❑
Could you outline its strategies if asked?	❑	❑
Are you aware of its precise objectives?	❑	❑
Have you checked out its purchasing plans lately?	❑	❑
Do you know what its production plans are?	❑	❑
Are you conscious of research and development plans?	❑	❑
Are you familiar with what is happening in the marketing department?	❑	❑
Could you descibe its market research plans on request?	❑	❑
Have you discovered its sales plans recently?	❑	❑
Do you know all about its financial plans?	❑	❑
Are you aware of what is occurring in the administration department?	❑	❑
Could you detail its personnel plans if necessary?	❑	❑
Would you be able to draw an organization chart for the firm?	❑	❑
Are you familiar with its current management practices?	❑	❑
Do you understand how the work is organized in each department?	❑	❑
Do you know how flexible the employees are with regard to working hours, methods and so on?	❑	❑
Could you outline productivity figures as and when requested?	❑	❑
Are you conscious of the equipment and machinery used in your concern?	❑	❑
Do you know how computerized your business is?	❑	❑
Do you recognize how technology is developing in your organization?	❑	❑
Do you realize how these factors can influence staff requirements both directly *and* indirectly?	❑	❑

Figure 8.1: A questionnaire about changing internal influences on staffing needs

happening to them at any given time. Accordingly, you should read the trade and business press, attend meetings, go to exhibitions and so on. Be aware of what is happening now in your trade and the wider business world, and how these changes and developments can affect your staff needs. The questionnaire shown in Figure 8.2 will help you judge if you are as familiar as you need to be.

Monitoring staffing levels   As with staff needs, you will have checked out your initial staffing levels when the personnel plan was to be implemented, recognized the probable internal and external changes which could occur during the life of the plan, and analyzed your forthcoming staffing levels as well; and consequently recruited with regard to them. Nonetheless, you must be attentive and stay in touch with the internal and external developments as and when they take place so that you can accommodate these and their knock-on effects within your plan.

Internal developments   At any particular moment, you should know precisely what is happening to the size and composition of the workforce. Do this by talking to colleagues, attending inter-departmental meetings and studying personnel records. Know when and why someone leaves, and whether it was anticipated or not, occurred earlier or later than expected and if it will have a roll-on effect on others in the firm. Figure 8.3 (page 118) is a questionnaire which will indicate if you know what is happening at present; if not, improvements have to be made.

External developments   Similarly, you have to understand the various external developments that are going on in the labour market, and which could affect the quality and quantity of your staffing levels. You do need to regularly liaise with job centre personnel, and read employment statistics and publications made available by such organizations as the Department of Employment. You should be conscious of labour shortages and gluts perhaps in different age groups, skills shortfalls and trends towards alternative approaches to work, such as flexi-time. The questionnaire shown as Figure 8.4 (page 119) will tell you if you are up-to-date with developments.

Maintaining the plan   Inevitably, your personnel plan will have to be amended and updated as time passes by: internal and external influences upon staff needs will be greater or lesser than expected whilst changes to staffing levels and developments in the labour market will be different from those which were anticipated originally. Accordingly, you should adjust your plan in line with the revised requirements and amended staffing levels.

You should be able to provide positive answers to all of the following questions. If you cannot, you may be out of touch with what is going on around you, and how it is influencing your staffing requirements.

	Yes	No
Do you know what is happening in your trade or industry?	❏	❏
Could you say if it were growing or declining, for example?	❏	❏
Are you aware of what your suppliers are doing?	❏	❏
Could you describe the availability of suppliers, supplies and the cost of materials?	❏	❏
Are you conscious of your competitors' activities?	❏	❏
Would you be able to state if they were growing or declining in number?	❏	❏
Individually, do you know which are expanding, merging or acquiring other firms?	❏	❏
Are you familiar with what is taking place in the economy?	❏	❏
Could you outline interest and inflation rates, as examples?	❏	❏
Could you detail employment and unemployment levels too?	❏	❏
Are you knowledgeable about the state?	❏	❏
Are you conversant with the policies of local, national and international governments?	❏	❏
Do you have a working knowledge of the law?	❏	❏
Are you aware of your trade body's codes of conduct and practice, for example?	❏	❏
Are you conscious of local, national and international legislation?	❏	❏
Do you know about the population?	❏	❏
Could you describe its age, structure, skills and attitudes, as examples?	❏	❏
Do you understand society?	❏	❏
Would you be able to explain its culture, customs and fashions?	❏	❏
Do you possess an appreciation of environmental issues?	❏	❏
In particular, could you state your company's environmental concerns?	❏	❏
Could you detail the environmental pressures upon it?	❏	❏
Do you know about the international marketplace?	❏	❏
Are you familiar with current exchange rates, import and export rules?	❏	❏
Are you aware of existing tariffs, embargoes, blockades, treaties and wars?	❏	❏
Do you realize how these factors influence your staffing needs both directly and indirectly?	❏	❏

Figure 8.2: A questionnaire about developing external influences on staffing needs

If you can respond positively to these questions, you probably have a sound understanding of what is happening within your workforce.

	Yes	No
Do you know exactly how many people are employed by your firm at the moment?	❏	❏
Are you aware of the numbers in each department?	❏	❏
Are you conscious of their respective grades and functions?	❏	❏
Do you know their ages and sex?	❏	❏
What about their skills, knowledge and experience?	❏	❏
How about their qualifications and lengths of service?	❏	❏
Do you know (a) who has just been recruited, (b) who is currently being recruited, (c) who is about to be recruited?	❏	❏
Are you aware of who is being trained and developed at present, and for which positions?	❏	❏
Do you know (a) who has just been transferred or promoted, (b) who is currently being transferred or promoted, (c) who is about to be transferred or promoted?	❏	❏
Are you concious of (a) who has just left, (b) who is in the process of leaving, (c) who is about to leave soon?	❏	❏
Do you know why they have left, or are leaving?	❏	❏
Could you update your personnel plan at present?	❏	❏
Could you compose an organizational chart at the moment?	❏	❏

Figure 8.3: A questionnaire about internal developments regarding staffing levels

Revised staff requirements   Never be afraid to revise the precise numbers and types of employees needed in the future; it would be unrealistic to expect to have made a wholly accurate estimate first time around. Be prepared to amend your requirements in terms of the total number for the organization and per department, the roles to be performed by each member of staff and the skills, knowledge and experience necessary in order to do those various jobs properly. Keep amending them too, typically on a quarterly basis, or sooner, if required.

Amended staffing levels   Do upgrade those personnel records which show the quantity and quality of staff employed by your firm: too often these are left months or even years out of date. In particular, keep scrupulous records of the numbers in total and by

---

You should be able to say 'Yes' to the following questions. If you can, it indicates that you know what is going on around you, and how it influences your workforce.

	Yes	No
Do you know whether the labour force is expanding or contracting?	❑	❑
Are you aware how its structure is changing?	❑	❑
With regard to young people and women, for example?	❑	❑
In relation to ethnic groups, self-employed and older people?	❑	❑
Are you conscious of the skills available within the labour force?	❑	❑
Do you know if there are skills shortfalls in certain occupations, trades, industries or regions?	❑	❑
Are you aware of skills gluts in key occupations, trades, industries or regions?	❑	❑
Are you familiar with changing attitudes to work?		
With regard to part-time, temporary and freelance work?	❑	❑
In relation to job sharing, flexi- and term time working?	❑	❑
Concerning working from home, career breaks and early retirement?	❑	❑
Do you know how it all affects you?	❑	❑

Figure 8.4: A questionnaire about external developments affecting staffing levels

---

department, grades and functions, age and sex, skills, knowledge, experiences, qualifications and length of employment. If you use an organization chart as part of your personnel plan, alter this carefully as well. Attend to these numerous matters as and when a recruitment, transfer promotion and/or departure takes place, or at least quarterly, as appropriate.

Matching staff requirements and levels Hopefully, as your personnel plan progresses and you become more experienced, the differences between staff requirements and levels will become minimal, if not non-existent. The key to continued success is simply hard work; conscientiously monitoring the influences upon requirements and calculating what these are as early as you can, and meticulously studying the changes and developments in levels and then manoeuvring these so that they match requirements as closely as possible.

SUMMARY   **1.** To develop a personnel plan, it is important that staff needs are evaluated on an ongoing basis, with particular attention being given to the internal and external influences upon these requirements.

2. Similarly, staffing levels must be monitored regularly, especially with regard to internal developments within the workforce and external developments in the labour market.

3. A personnel plan can be maintained if staff requirements and levels are amended and updated as often as possible. Consequently, levels can be adjusted to match requirements precisely, as time goes by.

Appendix A

Equal Opportunities Commission:
Code of Practice

RECRUITMENT

12. It is unlawful: UNLESS THE JOB IS COVERED BY AN EXCEPTION TO DISCRIMINATE DIRECTLY OR INDIRECTLY ON THE GROUNDS OF SEX OR MARRIAGE
    - IN THE ARRANGEMENTS MADE FOR DECIDING WHO SHOULD BE OFFERED A JOB.
    - IN ANY TERMS OF EMPLOYMENT.
    - BY REFUSING OR OMITTING TO OFFER A PERSON EMPLOYMENT.

13. It is therefore recommended that:
    (a) each individual should be assessed according to his or her personal capability to carry out a given job. It should not be assumed that men only or women only will be able to perform certain kinds of work;
    (b) any qualifications or requirements applied to a job which effectively inhibit applications from one sex or from married people should be retained only if they are justifiable in terms of the job to be done;
    (c) any age limits should be retained only if they are necessary for the job. An unjustifiable age limit could constitute unlawful indirect discrimination, for example, against women who have taken time out of employment for child-rearing;
    (d) where trade unions uphold such qualifications or requirements as union policy, they should amend that policy in the light of any potentially unlawful effect.

GENUINE OCCUPATION QUALIFICATIONS (GOQs)

14. It is unlawful: EXCEPT FOR CERTAIN JOBS WHEN A PERSON'S SEX IS A GENUINE OCCU-PATIONAL QUALIFICATION (GOQ) FOR THAT JOB to select candidates on the ground of sex.

15. There are very few instances in which a job will qualify for a GOQ on the ground of sex. However, exceptions may arise, for example, where considerations of privacy and decency or authenticity are involved. The SDA expressly states that the need of the job for strength and stamina does not justify restricting to men. When a GOQ exists for a job, it applies also to promotion, transfer, or training for that job, but cannot be used to justify a dismissal.

16. In some instances, the GOQ will apply to some of the duties only. A GOQ will not be valid, however, where members of the appropriate sex are already employed in sufficient numbers to meet the employer's likely requirements without undue inconvenience. For example, in a job where sales assistants may be required to undertake changing room duties, it might not be lawful to claim a GOQ in respect of all the assistants on the grounds that any of them might be required to undertake changing room duties from time to time.

17. It is therefore recommended that:
    - A job for which a GOQ was used in the past should be re-examined if the post falls vacant to see whether the GOQ still applies. Circumstances may well have changed, rendering the GOQ inapplicable.

SOURCES OF RECRUITMENT

18. It is unlawful: UNLESS THE JOB IS COVERED BY AN EXCEPTION:
    - TO DISCRIMINATE ON GROUNDS OF SEX OR MARRIAGE IN THE ARRANGEMENTS MADE FOR DETERMINING WHO SHOULD BE OFFERED EMPLOYMENT WHETHER RECRUITING BY ADVERTISEMENTS, THROUGH EMPLOYMENT AGENCIES, JOB-CENTRES, OR CAREER OFFICES.
    - TO IMPLY THAT APPLICATIONS FROM ONE SEX OR FROM MARRIED PEOPLE WILL NOT BE CONSIDERED.
    - TO INSTRUCT OR PUT PRESSURE ON OTHERS TO OMIT TO REFER FOR EMPLOYMENT PEOPLE OF ONE SEX OR MARRIED PEOPLE UNLESS THE JOB IS COVERED BY AN EXCEPTION.

    It is also unlawful WHEN ADVERTISING JOB VACANCIES,
    - TO PUBLISH OR CAUSE TO BE PUBLISHED AN ADVERTISEMENT WHICH INDICATES OR MIGHT REASONABLY BE UNDERSTOOD AS INDICATING AN INTENTION TO DISCRIMINATE UNLAWFULLY ON GROUNDS OF SEX OR MARRIAGE.

19. It is therefore recommended that:

    Advertising
    (a) job advertising should be carried out in such a way to encourage applications from suitable candidates of both sexes. This can be achieved both by wording of the advertisements and, for example, by placing advertisements in publications likely to reach both sexes. All advertising material and accompanying literature relating to employment or training issues should be reviewed to ensure that it avoids presenting men and women in stereotyped roles. Such stereotyping tends to perpetuate sex segregation in jobs and can also lead people of the opposite sex to believe that they would be unsuccessful in applying for particular jobs;
    (b) where vacancies are filled by promotion or transfer, they should be published to all eligible employees in such a way that they do not restrict applications from either sex;
    (c) recruitment solely or primarily by word of mouth may unnecessarily restrict the choice of applicants available. The method should be avoided in a workforce predominantly of one sex, if in practice it prevents members of the opposite sex from applying;

(d) where applicants are supplied through trade unions and members of one sex only come forward, this should be discussed with the unions and an alternative approach adopted.

Careers Service/Schools
20. When notifying vacancies to the Careers Service, employers should specify that these are open to both boys and girls. This is especially important when a job has traditionally been done exclusively or mainly by one sex. If dealing with single-sex schools, they should ensure, where possible, that both boys' and girls' schools are approached; it is also a good idea to remind mixed schools that jobs are open to boys and girls.

SELECTION METHODS

Tests
21. (a) If selection tests are used, they should be specifically related to job and/or career requirements and should measure an individual's actual or inherent ability to do or train for the work or career.
    (b) Tests should be reviewed regularly to ensure that they remain relevant and free from any unjustifiable bias, either in content or in scoring mechanism.

Applications and Interviewing
22. It is unlawful: UNLESS THE JOB IS COVERED BY AN EXCEPTION:
TO DISCRIMINATE ON GROUNDS OF SEX OR MARRIAGE BY REFUSING OR DELIBERATELY OMITTING TO OFFER EMPLOYMENT.

23. It is therefore recommended that:
    (a) employers should ensure that personnel staff, line managers and all other employees who may come into contact with job applicants, should be trained in the provisions of the SDA, including the fact that it is unlawful to instruct or put pressure on others to discriminate;
    (b) applications from men and women should be processed in exactly the same way. For example, there should not be separate lists of male and female or married and single applicants. All those handling applications and conducting interviews should be trained in the avoidance of unlawful discrimination and records of interviews kept, where practicable, showing why applicants were or were not appointed;
    (c) questions should relate to the requirements of the job. Where it is necessary to assess whether personal circumstances will affect performance of the job (for example, where it involves unsocial hours or extensive travel) this should be discussed objectively without detailed questions based on assumptions about marital status, children and domestic obligations. Questions about marriage plans or family intentions should not be asked, as they could be construed as showing bias against women. Information necessary for personnel records can be collected after a job offer has been made.

PROMOTION, TRANSFER AND TRAINING

24. It is unlawful: UNLESS THE JOB IS COVERED BY AN EXCEPTION, FOR EMPLOYERS TO DISCRIMINATE DIRECTLY OR INDIRECTLY ON THE GROUND OF SEX OR MARRIAGE IN THE WAY THEY AFFORD ACCESS TO OPPORTUNITIES FOR PROMOTION, TRANSFER OR TRAINING.

25. It is therefore recommended that:
    (a) where an appraisal system is in operation, the assessment criteria should be examined to ensure that they are not unlawfully discriminatory and the scheme monitored to assess how it is working in practice;
    (b) when a group of workers predominantly of one sex is excluded from an appraisal scheme, access to promotion, transfer and training and to other benefits should be reviewed, to ensure that there is no unlawful indirect discrimination;
    (c) promotion and career development patterns are reviewed to ensure that the traditional qualifications are justifiable requirements for the job to be done. In some circumstances, for example, promotion on the basis of length of service could amount to unlawful indirect discrimination, as it may unjustifiably affect more women than men;
    (d) when general ability and personal qualities are the main requirements for promotion to a post, care should be taken to consider favourably candidates of both sexes with differing career patterns and general experience;
    (e) rules which restrict or preclude transfer between certain jobs should be questioned and changed if they are found to be unlawfully discriminatory. Employees of one sex may be concentrated in sections from which transfers are traditionally restricted without real justification;
    (f) policies and practices regarding selection for training, day release and personal development should be examined for unlawful direct and indirect discrimination. Where there is found to be an imbalance in training as between sexes, the cause should be identified to ensure that it is not discriminatory;
    (g) age limits for access to training and promotion should be questioned.

(Extract reproduced by kind permission of the Equal Opportunities Commission)

Appendix B

Commission for Racial Equality:
Code of Practice

RECRUITMENT, PROMOTION, TRANSFER, TRAINING & DISMISSAL

Sources of Recruitment

Advertisements

1.5 *When advertising job vacancies it is unlawful for employers:*
to publish an advertisement which indicates, or could reasonably be understood as indicating, an intention to discriminate against applicants from a particular racial group.

1.6 It is therefore recommended that:
   a) employers should not confine advertisements unjustifiably to those areas or publications which would exclude or disproportionately reduce the numbers of applicants of a particular racial group;
   b) employers should avoid prescribing requirements such as length of residence or experience in the UK and where a particular qualification is required it should be made clear that a fully comparable qualification obtained overseas is as acceptable as a UK qualification.

1.7 In order to demonstrate their commitment to equality of opportunity it is recommended that where employers send literature to applicants, this should include a statement that they are equal opportunity employers.

Employment Agencies

1.8 *When recruiting through employment agencies, job centres, careers offices and schools, it is unlawful for employers:*
   a) *to give instructions to discriminate for example by indicating that certain groups will or will not be preferred. (For exceptions see the Race Relations Act);*
   b) *to bring pressure on them to discriminate against members of a particular racial group. (For exceptions, as above).*

1.9 In order to avoid indirect discrimination it is recommended that employers should not confine recruitment unjustifiably to those agencies, job centres, careers offices and schools which, because of their particular source of applicants, provide only or mainly applicants of a particular racial group.

Other Sources

1.10 *It is unlawful to use recruitment methods which exclude or disproportionately reduce the numbers of applicants of a particular racial group and which cannot be shown to be justifiable.* It is therefore recommended that employers should not recruit through the following methods:

a) recruitment, solely or in the first instance, through the recommendations of existing employees where the workforce concerned is wholly or predominantly white or black and the labour market is multi-racial;

b) procedures by which applicants are mainly or wholly supplied through trade unions where this means that only members of a particular racial group, or a disproportionately high number of them, come forward.

Sources for Promotion and Training

1.11 *It is unlawful for employers to restrict access to opportunities for promotion or training in a way which is discriminatory.* It is therefore recommended that:

- job and training vacancies and the application procedure should be made known to all eligible employees, and not in such a way as to exclude or disproportionately reduce the numbers of applicants from a particular racial group.

SELECTION FOR RECRUITMENT, PROMOTION, TRANSFER, TRAINING AND DISMISSAL

1.12 *It is unlawful to discriminate,* not only in recruitment promotion transfer and training but also in the arrangements made for recruitment and in the ways of affording access to opportunities for promotion transfer or training.*

Selection Criteria and Tests

1.13 In order to avoid direct or indirect discrimination it is recommended that selection criteria and tests are examined to ensure that they are related to job requirements and are not unlawfully discriminatory. For example:

a) a standard of English higher than that needed for the safe and effective performance of the job or clearly demonstrable career pattern should not be required, or a higher level of educational qualification than is needed;

b) in particular, employers should not disqualify applicants because they are unable to complete an application form unassisted unless personal completion of the form is a valid test of the standard of English required for safe and effective performance of the job;

c) overseas degrees, diplomas and other qualifications which are comparable with UK qualifications should be accepted as equivalents, and not simply be assumed to be of an inferior quality;

d) selection tests which contain irrelevant questions or exercises on matters which may be unfamiliar to racial minority applicants should not be used (for example, general knowledge questions on matters more likely to be familiar to indigenous applicants);

e) selection tests should be checked to ensure that they are related to the job's requirements, i.e. an individual's test markings should measure ability to do or train for the job in question.

* It should be noted that discrimination in selection to achieve 'racial balance' is not allowed. The clause in the 1968 Race Relations Act which allowed such discrimination for the purpose of securing or preserving a reasonable balance of persons of different racial groups in the establishment is not included in the 1976 Race Relations Act.

Treatment of Applicants, Shortlisting, Interviewing and Selection

1.14 In order to avoid direct or indirect discrimination it is recommended that:

a) gate, reception and personnel staff should be instructed not to treat casual or formal applicants from particular racial groups less favourably than others. These instructions should be confirmed in writing;

b) in addition, staff responsible for shortlisting, interviewing and selecting candidates should be:
   – clearly informed of selection criteria and of the need for their consistent application;
   – given guidance or training on the effects which generalised assumptions and prejudices about race can have on selection decisions;
   – made aware of the possible misunderstandings that can occur in interviews between persons of different cultural background;

c) wherever possible, shortlisting and interviewing should not be done by one person alone but should at least be checked at a more senior level.

Genuine Occupational Qualification

1.15 *Selection on racial grounds is allowed in certain jobs where being of a particular group is a genuine occupational qualification for that job.* An example is where the holder of a particular job provides persons of a racial group with personal services promoting their welfare, and those services can most effectively be provided by a person of that group.

Transfers and Training

1.16 In order to avoid direct or indirect discrimination it is recommended that:

a) staff responsible for selecting employees for transfer to other jobs should be instructed to apply selection criteria without unlawful discrimination;

b) industry or company agreements and arrangements of custom and practice on job transfers should be examined and amended if they are found to contain requirements or conditions which appear to be indirectly discriminatory. For example, if employees of a particular racial group are concentrated in particular sections, the transfer arrangements should be examined to see if they are unjustifiably and unlawfully restrictive and amended if necessary;

c) staff responsible for selecting employees for training, whether induction, promotion or skill training should be instructed not to discriminate on racial grounds;

d) selection criteria for training opportunities should be examined to ensure that they are not indirectly discriminatory.

(Extract reproduced by kind permission of the Commission for Racial Equality.)

Appendix C

Department of Employment:
Code of Good Practice on the Employment of
Disabled People

RECRUITING PEOPLE WITH DISABILITIES –
THE RECRUITMENT AND SELECTION PROCESS

5.1 If people with disabilities are to obtain opportunities within your company according to their abilities, then it is important that you use recruitment methods which encourage applicants with disabilities. It is also important to ensure that your application and selection procedures do not discourage or exclude people with disabilities because they have a disability. This section describes some ways of ensuring that you attract applications from suitable people with disabilities and that your application and selection procedures are fair to these workers.

Job descriptions and job requirements

5.2 Whatever your recruitment methods, remember when drawing up job descriptions that certain job requirements may inadvertently exclude people with disabilities more so than other applicants. It is therefore important to check that job requirements are strictly related to the needs of the job. For instance, avoid where possible the setting of unnecessarily rigid age limits as unemployed people with disabilities tend to be older than other workers. Where job requirements are flexible, make this clear in the job description. For example, to require applicants to have a driving licence when the ability to drive is only occasionally useful rather than essential could well exclude some suitable applicants with disabilities, e.g. blind people.

Methods of recruitment –
ways of encouraging suitable people with disabilities to apply for your jobs

5.3 Your company will have sources of recruitment appropriate to its own needs. However, if the number of people with disabilities it employs is to increase, you will need to know of the methods of recruitment well placed to put you in touch with people with disabilities interested in your vacancies. These are:
- staff at your local Jobcentre, including the Disablement Resettlement Officer;
- the specialist careers officer or other staff at your local careers office;
- special schools, or special units for people with disabilities within ordinary schools. Consider building links with these. A good example is a firm making high precision instruments which, in a workforce of 100, employs 20 people

with disabilities. Most of these were recruited from a local special school and some have been with the firm for over 20 years;

- organisations for people with disabilities in your area;
- other organisations which can put you in touch with suitable candidates with disabilities.

Advertising vacancies in the press

5.4   If your company advertises vacancies in the press, a short statement in the advertisement that applications from people with disabilities are welcome will:

- help to ensure that your company is recognised as one which offers fair opportunities to people with disabilities;
- encourage suitable workers with disabilities to apply.

Other methods of recruitment

5.5   If you use other methods of recruitment, such as private agencies or informal contacts, let it be known that applications from people with disabilities are welcome.

Application and selection procedures

5.6   The aim of any selection process will be to ensure that you get the right people for the job. To do that you will look at their abilities, experience and likely commitment. This is exactly what you should do for applicants with disabilities. However, you will also need to know about any disability which is relevant to the job in question. This will help you to make a full assessment and to consider whether any special help is needed.

5.7   Many people with disabilities are quite prepared to give details of their disability. Others may be unwilling to divulge such information for a number of reasons:

- they believe the disability has no effect on ability to do the job in question and is thus not relevant to the job application;
- there may be a fear that if a disability which is not immediately apparent is revealed (e.g. a history of epileptic attacks at work) an interview will not be granted, irrespective of ability to do the job.

5.8   It is therefore important for your company to consider carefully the circumstances in which it needs to know about any disability and the use it makes of this information. You will do much to reassure workers with disabilities if you make it clear on application forms, during interviews or in connection with health screening and medical checks that disability does not preclude full consideration for the job.

Application forms

5.9   Give some extra thought to the wording of application forms – a considerable amount of professional personnel expertise exists in this field. A positive approach would be to preface any questions about health or disability with a statement that the company welcomes applications from suitable people with disabilities and that all information is treated as confidential.

5.10 An example of an appropriately worded statement is: *a disability or health problem does not preclude full consideration for the job and applications from suitable people with disabilities are welcome. All information provided by applicants will be treated as confidential.*

5.11 Examples of appropriately worded questions are:
   1. *Do you have a health problem, or a disability, which is relevant to our job application?*
   2. *If yes, please describe the health problem or disability in this space.*
   3. *If yes, are you registered as disabled with the Jobcentre (do you hold a green card)?*
5.12 Where your company has access to occupational medical or nursing advice, detailed questioning on health may need to be covered in a separate health questionnaire. This should be seen only by occupational health staff and relevant information it contains given only to personnel, managerial or supervisory staff concerned with the application.

Interviewing candidates
5.13 Application forms often only give simplified information and a brief picture. The only realistic and effective means of assessing the employment potential of workers with disabilities may be through interviews. You should consider therefore inviting all suitably qualified candidates with disabilities for interview, particularly if your company employs only a small number of people with disabilities or does not fulfil quota.

Practical interview arrangements
5.14 In the case of some people with disabilities, special arrangements for interviews may be needed and, where appropriate, invitations to interview could ask if this is the case. Examples of such arrangements are:
   - allowing deaf or speech-impaired people to bring an interpreter if they wish (a special service exists which can arrange for an interpreter);
   - alerting staff to be prepared to show blind people to the place of interview;
   - allowing mentally handicapped people to bring a friend or relative to assist when answering questions;
   - ensuring that the place of interview is accessible to any candidate with a mobility problem, or that assistance is available to help them on arrival.
5.15 In addition to the normal preparations which you make for interviewing all workers, it may be helpful to gain some prior knowledge of any disability and possible handicap which may have to be discussed. If the candidate has been referred by Jobcentre staff, then they may be able to give you relevant information. The Employers Guide to Disabilities, published by Woodhead Faulkner in conjunction with the Royal Association for Disability and Rehabilitation, provides concise and helpful information.

The interview itself
5.16 Most candidates at interviews are likely to be nervous. People with disabilities particularly so because of past experiences where they consider employers had been unable to look beyond their disabilities. Try, therefore, to put candidates with disabilities more at their ease by emphasising that disability does not affect the consideration they will receive. You will of course want to discuss any possible handicap fully and objectively, but do not make assumptions about what a candidate with a disability, for instance someone with a physical handicap, can or cannot do. The interview should concentrate on the person's abilities and if possible provide an opportunity for these to be demonstrated, e.g. manual dexterity.

Health screening
5.17 Health checks, whether short health screening checks or full medical examinations, are by no means necessary in the case of all jobs, nor are they necessary in the case of all people with disabilities. Your company will no doubt have its own policy with regard to health screening, and people with disabilities should be considered in the same way as other people within that policy.
5.18 People with disabilities should not be excluded from jobs because it is thought that health screening will automatically lead to their rejection.
5.19 However, it is important also that you do not reject a candidate with a disability on the basis of doubts about such things as fitness, safety or the severity of a handicap when health checks or a medical examination could dispel such doubts. If you need advice, the Employment Medical Advisory Service of the Health and Safety Executive will advise you on the desirability of health checks in particular instances before employment is offered and has published a guidance note on pre-employment health screening.

The Job Introduction Scheme
5.20 If you are still unsure about a disabled worker's ability to do a particular job, ask the local Jobcentre about the Job Introduction Scheme. This Scheme provides financial assistance through the Employment Service to enable you to take a worker with a disability on trial.
5.21 Similar assistance is also available through the Pathway Scheme run by the Royal Society for Mentally Handicapped Children and Adults (MENCAP). This Scheme, which runs alongside the Job Introduction Scheme, is gradually being introduced nationwide. It provides grants to the employer and to a fellow worker to encourage the recruitment and training of mentally handicapped people.

(Extract reproduced by kind permission of the Department of Employment.)

Useful contacts

These organisations can provide information and guidance in their respective fields, on request. Most publish a range of leaflets and booklets which will be of relevance to you; some of these are available free of charge, on receipt of a large, stamp addressed envelope.

British Psychological Society, St Andrew's House, 48 Princess Road East, Lancaster, LE1 7DR. Tel: 01533 549568.

BUPA Medical Centres Limited, Webb House, 210 Pentonville Road, London W1. Tel: 0171 837 8641.

Commission for Racial Equality, Elliot House, 10–12 Allington Street, London SW1E 5EH Tel: 0171 828 7022.

Criterion Partnership*, 6 Offham Terrace, Parkview, Lewes, East Sussex BN7 2QP. Tel: 01273 480583.

Department of Employment, Caxton House, Tothill Street, London SW1H 9HF. Tel: 0171 273 3000.

And at: Chesser House West, 502 Gorgie Road, Edinburgh EH11 3YH. Tel: 0131 443 8731.

Department of Trade and Industry, Ashdown House, 123 Victoria Street, London SW1E 6RB. Tel: 0171 215 5000.

Employment Service, St Vincent House, 30 Orange Street, London WC2 7HT. Tel: 0171 839 5600.

Equal Opportunities Commission, Overseas House, Quay Street, Manchester M3 3HN. Tel: 0161 833 9244.

And at: Caerwys House, Windsor Lane, Cardiff, CF1 1LB. Tel: 01222 343552.

And at: Stock Exchange House, 7 Nelson Mandela Place, Glasgow G2 1QW. Tel: 0141 248 5833.

European Union Information Office, 8 Storey's Gate, London SW1P 3AT. Tel: 0171 973 1992.

Educational and Industrial Test Services Limited*, 83 High Street, Hemel Hampstead, Hertfordshire HP1 3AH. Tel: 01442 256773.

Hodder and Stoughton*, PO Box 702, Dunton Green, Sevenoaks, Kent TN13 2YD. Tel: 01732 450111.

Knight Chapman Pyschological Limited*, 48 High Street, Lewes, East Sussex BN7 2DD. Tel: 01273 417535.

NFER-Nelson Publishing Company Limited*, Darville House, 2 Oxford Road East, Windsor, Berkshire SL4 1DF. Tel: 01753 850333.

PPP Medical Centre, 99 New Cavendish Street, London W1M 3FQ. Tel: 0171 637 8941.

Opportunities for the Disabled, 1 Bank Buildings, Princes Street, London EC2R 8EW. Tel: 0171 726 4961.

Oxford Psychologists Press*, Lambourne House, 311–321 Banbury Road, Oxford OX2 7JH. Tel: 01865 510203.

Psychological Corporation Limited*, Foots Cray High Street, Sidcup, Kent DA14 5HP. Tel: 0181 300 3322.

Psytech International Limited*, Icknield House, Eastcheap, Letchworth, Hertfordshire, SG6 3DA. Tel: 01462 482833.

Royal Association for Disability and Rehabilitation, 25 Mortimer Street, London W1N 8AB. Tel: 0171 637 5400.

Savile and Holdsworth Limited*, 3 AC Court, High Street, Thames Ditton, Surrey KT7 0SR. Tel: 0181 398 4170.

Selby Mill Smith Limited*, 30 Circus Mews, Bath, Avon BA1 2PW. Tel: 01225 446655.

The Test Agency*, Cournswood House, North Dean, High Wycombe, Buckinghamshire HP14 4NW. Tel: 01494 563384.

*Publishers and/or distributors of psychological tests.

Recommended reading

The following books are all worth reading as they will help to increase your knowledge and understanding of the key aspects of introducing and developing an effective personnel plan. You should be able to obtain them from your local bookshop, or library.

Chapter 1: Introducing a personnel plan
Hollinshead G., and Leat, M., *Human Resource Systems*, Pitman Publishing, London, 1994.
Tyson, S., *Human Resource Strategy*, Pitman Publishing, London, 1994.

Chapter 2: Studying existing vacancies
Clements, P., and Spinks, T., *The Equal Opportunities Guide*, Kogan Page, London, 1994.
Malone, M., *Discrimination Law*, Kogan Page, London, 1993.

Chapter 3: Looking for applicants
Coutis, J., *Recruitment Advertising*, Institute of Personnel and Development, London, 1994.
Maitland, I., *How to Plan Press Advertising*, Cassell, London, 1996.
Maitland, I., *How to Plan Radio Advertising*, Cassell, London, 1996.

Chapter 4: Shortlisting applicants
Bird, P., *Tame that Phone!*, Pitman Publishing, London, 1994.
Cochrane, P., *The Power of the Phone*, Pitman Publishing, London, 1993.

Chapter 5: Interviewing candidates
Fletcher, J., *Conducting Effective Interviews*, Kogan Page, London, 1995.
Honey, P., *Face to Face*, Gower, Aldershot, 1988.
Peel, M., *Readymade Interview Questions*, Kogan Page, London 1988.
Rae, L., *The Skills of Interviewing*, Gower, Aldershot, 1989.

Chapter 6: Testing candidates
Barrett, J., and Williams, G., *Test Your Own Aptitude*, Kogan Page, London, 1995.
Edenborough, R., *Using Psychometrics*, Kogan Page, London, 1994.
Jones, J. W., *Personnel Testing*, Kogan Page, London, 1995.
Maitland, I., *How to Win at Aptitude Tests*, Thorsons, London, 1997.

Chapter 7: Selecting employees
Skeats, J., *Successful Induction*, Kogan Page, London, 1991.
Waud, C., *Employment Law 1995*, Kogan Page, London, 1995.

Chapter 8: Developing a personnel plan
McManus, J., *The Perfect Dismissal*, Random House, London, 1993.
Reay, D. G., *Selecting Training Methods*, Kogan Page, London, 1994.
Toulson, N., *Preparing Staff for Recruitment*, Gower, Aldershot, 1994.

Glossary

Aptitude tests. Tests to assess a candidate's specific aptitudes, such as manual dexterity. Also known as special ability tests.

Board interviews. See panel interviews.

Closed questions. Questions which tend to produce only a 'yes' or 'no' response. As an example, 'Do you live at 5 Thomas Avenue, Trimley?'
Contra indicators. Negative features listed on person specifications which would discount candidates who possessed them from further consideration for the job.
Curricula vitae. Documents summarizing an applicant's personal and work history.

Direct discrimination. Discrimination of an obvious nature. As an example, an advertisement which read 'Wanted – Workmen for Building Site'.
Discrimination. Inequitable treatment, usually relating to sex, marital status, race, age or perceived sexual preferences.

Employee specifications. See person specifications.
Employment agencies. Agencies which tend to recruit staff for lower level posts. Some specialize in particular areas: computer and secretarial staff, as examples.

General aptitude tests. See intelligence tests.

Genuine occupational qualifications. Sex or race related selection criteria which are permissible because of the particular features of the job. As an example, a female person may be sought to work as an attendant in a women's toilets and shower area; on the grounds of decency and privacy.
Group tests. Tests which involve all candidates working together; usually to resolve a problem. Candidates are monitored and assessed as they work.

Hypothetical questions. Questions which focus on imaginary situations. For example, 'What would you do if a customer threatened you?'

Indirect discrimination. Less obvious discrimination which exists in recruitment when requirements or conditions are set which tend to favour one group more than another. For example, weight requirements might be specified; and women tend to be lighter; men heavier.
Induction. The process of settling a recruit into a job as efficiently and as effectively as possible.
Intelligence tests. Tests which incorporate questions designed to assess various aspects of a candidate's general intelligence. Also called general aptitude tests and mental ability tests.

IQ tests. See intelligence tests.

Job analysis. The systematic process of accumulating information about and appraising all aspects of a given job.

Job descriptions. Documents which outline the main purpose, tasks and responsibilities of a job.

Job specifications. See person specifications.

Leading questions. Questions which suggest what the 'right' answer would be; and therefore, should not be asked. For example, 'Are you enthusiastic?'

Limited questions. Questions which tend to produce a limited response. As an example, 'Who was your boss at Grisbys?'

Manpower plans. See personnel plans.

Mental ability tests. See intelligence tests.

Multiple questions. Questions comprising several associated questions all rolled into one. For example, 'Do you like reading? What's your favourite newspaper? Do you read the trade press?'

Non-verbal ability tests. Tests which include questions involving symbols. Designed to assess a candidate's ability to differentiate between relevant and irrelevant data.

Numerical ability tests. Tests which consist of questions using numbers. Designed to assess a candidate's ability with figures.

One-to-one interviews. Interviews comprising one interviewer and one interviewee.

Open questions. Questions which encourage candidates to talk freely. For example, 'What did you do in that job?'

Panel interviews. Interviews comprising two or more interviewers and one interviewee. Also known as board interviews.

Person specifications. Documents which set out the skills, knowledge and experience needed to do a particular job properly. Also called employee, job or personnel specifications.

Personality tests. Tests designed to assess the 'real' person behind the candidate.

Personnel plans. Schemes whereby current and future staffing needs and levels are identified and worked towards with a view to ensuring they are matched as precisely as possible.

Personnel specifications. See person specifications.

Problem-solving activities. Activities of a group nature whereby candidates have to work together in order to resolve job and/or trade related problems.

Recruitment agencies. Agencies which tend to concentrate on recruiting people for management posts.

Search consultants. Specialists who headhunt people for senior positions in organizations.

Spatial ability tests. Tests incorporating questions which use shapes. Designed to evaluate a candidate's ability to think visually.

Special ability tests. See aptitude tests.

Statements of employment. See written statements of employment.

Unlawful discrimination. See discrimination.

Verbal ability tests. Tests containing questions which involve words. Designed to assess a candidate's verbal ability and understanding of verbal concepts.

Written statements of employment. Documents specifying the main terms and conditions of employment.

Index